Bacon's Rebellion, 1676–1677

REACTING TO THE PAST is an award-winning series of immersive role-playing games that actively engage students in their own learning. Students assume the roles of historical characters and practice critical thinking, primary source analysis, and argument, both written and spoken. Reacting games are flexible enough to be used across the curriculum, from first-year general education classes and discussion sections of lecture classes to capstone experiences, intersession courses, and honors programs.

Reacting to the Past was originally developed under the auspices of Barnard College and is sustained by the Reacting Consortium of colleges and universities. The Consortium hosts a regular series of conferences and events to support faculty and administrators.

NOTE TO INSTRUCTORS: Before beginning the game you must download the game materials, including an instructor's manual containing a detailed schedule of class sessions, role sheets for students, and handouts.

To download these essential resources, visit https://reactingconsortium.org/games, click on the page for this title, then click "Game Materials."

Bacon's Rebellion, 1676–1677

RACE, CLASS, AND FRONTIER CONFLICT IN COLONIAL VIRGINIA

VERDIS LEVAR ROBINSON
AND PAUL OTTO

REACTING TO THE PAST

BARNARD

The University of North Carolina Press

Chapel Hill

© 2024 Reacting Consortium, Inc.
All rights reserved
Manufactured in the United States of America

Cover art: Howard Pyle, *The Burning of Jamestown* (1905). Courtesy Wikimedia Commons.

ISBN 978-1-4696-7892-4 (pbk.: alk. paper)
ISBN 978-1-4696-7893-1 (epub)
ISBN 979-8-8908-8741-2 (pdf)

Contents

List of Illustrations / ix

1. INTRODUCTION / 1

Brief Overview of the Game / 1

   A Note about Nomenclature / 3

Prologue: My Brother's Keeper? / 4

Basic Features of Reacting to the Past / 7

   Game Setup / 7

   Game Play / 7

   Game Requirements / 8

   Controversy / 8

2. HISTORICAL BACKGROUND / 11

Chronology / 11

"Most Excellent Fruits": A Historical Overview of Colonial Virginia to 1676 / 12

   Introduction / 12

   "Great & Ample": Creating Virginia / 14

   "Our Late Reconsiled Salvage Enymies": Anglo–Native American Relations in Colonial Virginia / 16

   "Masterless Men": Creating Anglo-Virginians / 18

   "20 and Odd Negroes": Creating Afro-Virginians / 20

   "The Governor, Council and Assembly": Government and Politics / 23

   "He That Lives in the Nature of a Servant": Virginia's Sociopolitical Hierarchy, Social Unrest, and Rising Tensions / 26

   "For the Lord's Sake Shoot No More, These Are Our Friends the Susquehannocks": Native American–Anglo Virginian Conflict, 1675–1676 / 29

3. THE GAME / 33

- Major Issues for Debate / 33
  - Defensive Approach / 33
  - Offensive Approach / 33
- Other Issues for Debate / 34
- Rules and Procedures / 35
  - Objectives and Victory Conditions / 35
  - The Grand Assembly / 35
  - Additional Rules of the Grand Assembly / 37
  - How to Join a Faction / 39
  - Militias / 39
  - The Smuggler / 40
  - The Gossiper / 41
  - Other Matters / 42
- Basic Outline of the Game / 43
  - Setup Sessions / 43
  - Social Session: The Calm before the Storm / 44
  - Part 1 (Legislative Session 1): "The Long Assembly," March 7, 1676 / 44
  - Subsequent Game Sessions / 45
  - Debriefing / 45
- Assignments / 46
  - Papers / 46
  - Speeches / 46
  - Grades / 46
- Counterfactuals / 46

4. ROLES AND FACTIONS / 49

- The Berkeleyan Faction / 49
- The Baconian Faction / 50
- Indeterminates / 51

5. CORE TEXTS / 55

- Note on the Texts / 55
  - John Rolfe, on the Arrival of African Slaves (1619) / 56
  - Virginia Laws Regarding Labor, Slavery, and Race (1619–1676) / 58
  - Anthony Johnson, A Former Slave Claims His Slave Property (1655) / 60
  - The Case of Elizabeth Key (1655–1656) / 61
  - Land Patent Book (circa 1650s) / 64
  - The Gloucester Conspiracy (1663) / 65
  - George Alsop, *A Character of the Province of Mary-Land* (1666) / 68
  - Lower Norfolk County Court Minutes (1667) / 70
  - Sir William Berkeley, "Enquiries to the Governor of Virginia from the Lords Commissioners of Foreign Plantations" (1671) / 70
  - Francis Payne, "A Free Negro Property Owner in Colonial Virginia Bequeaths His Property" (1673) / 74
  - Council Minutes (1674) / 75
  - Thomas Mathew, "The Beginning, Progress, and Conclusion of Bacon's Rebellion, 1675–1676" (1705) / 76
  - John Easton, "A Relation of the Indian War" (1675) / 77
  - *"The History of Bacon's and Ingram's Rebellion in Virginia, and in 1676"* / 80
- Supplemental Texts / 83
  - "A True Narrative of the Late Rebellion in Virginia, by the Royal Commissioners" (1677) / 83
  - Edward Randolph, "The Causes and Results of King Philip's War" (1685) / 84

Robert Beverly, *The History and Present State of Virginia* (1705) / 86

"The History of Bacon's and Ingram's Rebellion in Virginia, and in 1676" / 87

Elizabeth Bacon, Letter to Her Sister in London (June 29, 1676) / 87

Philip Ludwell, "An Account of the Rebellious Mutiny Raised by Nathanial Bacon" (1676) / 88

Thomas Ludwell and Robert Smith, "Proposals for Reducing the Rebels in Virginia to Their Obedience" (1676) / 90

King Charles II, "A Proclamation for the Suppressing of a Rebellion Lately Raised Within the Plantation of Virginia" (1676) / 90

Royal Commissioners' Narrative (1677) / 91

Anna Cotton, "An Account of Our Late Troubles in Virginia" (1676) / 92

Virginia Laws Regarding Labor, Slavery, and Race: Acts I, II, and X (1679–1682) / 97

Acknowledgments / 99

Appendix: March Assembly Proposal / 101

Notes / 103

Selected Bibliography / 105

Illustrations

MAP

2.1 The Colony of Virginia in 1675 / 13

FIGURES

2.1 The Third Statehouse, Jamestown, ca. 1675 / 25

2.2 Virginia's social and political hierarchy / 26

2.3 Sketch of Susquehannock fort and siege by an English observer / 31

3.1 Recommended classroom layout / 36

TABLES

2.1 North American colonies, 1565–1670 / 14

2.2 Virginia statutes concerning race, 1630–1672 / 22

2.3 Tudor and Stuart monarchs of England, 1558–1685 / 24

3.1 Characters with voting power / 39

Bacon's Rebellion, 1676–1677

1
Introduction

BRIEF OVERVIEW OF THE GAME

Exactly 100 years before the Founding Fathers signed the Declaration of Independence, a civil war broke out in Virginia that sent shockwaves through the English colonies and whose ripples could be felt across the Atlantic in England itself. Once regarded by historians as a precursor to the American Revolution, Bacon's Rebellion symbolized to them the patriots' enlightened revolutionary ideals through a premature uprising against the tyranny of hierarchical rule. However, modern scholars argue in favor of an approach that focuses more on America's original sin—slavery. In this telling, Bacon's Rebellion became a focal point in colonial Virginia in the transformation from a society with slaves to a slave society.

In the early seventeenth century, a multiracial society emerged in the Chesapeake region where tobacco had become a wildly successful cash crop. Native Americans, Africans, and Europeans coexisted in a variety of ways: they worked together, played together, drank together, procreated with each other, fought side by side, and died together. However, as the population grew through immigration and reproduction, a hierarchical order developed in Virginia and Maryland in which a small few individuals occupied the highest rungs of society, exercising significant economic, social, and political power, while the majority resided on the lowest rungs. Those on the top controlled the majority of the land, labor, and profits. Through colony-wide and local political office, they ruled Virginia, while those on the bottom were landless, relegated to the frontier (land not in possession of the colonial elite), and without influence in colonial governance. Many of these landless had come to Virginia as indentured servants, as most English did in the seventeenth century. A lucky few of those who outlived their terms of service acquired land and achieved varying degrees of financial success and social advancement. But increasingly, the freedmen found it impossible to establish themselves as independent landowners. Meanwhile, enslaved Africans were being imported to the colony. While their status was sometimes ambiguous and the rare individual did achieve freedom for themselves and their families, the status of Africans degraded over the seventeenth century, reducing the rare opportunities that had earlier existed.

Even among the highest rungs of society, there were divisions. Friends of the governor, Sir William Berkeley, held the most power. Those outside his inner circle were often disappointed in their aspirations for greater wealth and power. Exacerbating this disaffection were falling tobacco prices and greater competition for a shrinking market. Manufactured goods from England increased in cost while war between England and the Netherlands cast a pall on the colony and its future.

Meanwhile, with more arrivals and growing numbers of men and women freed from terms of service, the Virginia frontier—where the far reaches of colonial settlement overlapped with Indian country creating a zone of intense intercultural contact—became a focal point of conflict and violence. As settler demand for land in Indian country increased, so too did settler deaths. After being mistakenly and unjustly attacked by colonists in the summer of 1675, displaced Susquehannocks avenged themselves on backcountry settlers, creating for the colony a major security issue. As 1676 opened, the colonial leadership faced a major crisis, but their blundering and uncertain response to that crisis combined with the underlying tensions in the colony laid the colony open to a civil war.

Nathaniel Bacon, nephew of Governor Berkeley and relative newcomer to the colony, arose as a champion of the disaffected, both the unlanded and unfree as well as the disaffected elite.

In essence, Bacon's Rebellion was a conflict within the colonial Virginia gentry—the elite planters rewarded for loyalty to the established order, but in disagreement over Virginia's governance. With a powerful elite class ever increasing their authority and landholdings, the lower classes of Anglo- and Afro-Virginians became increasingly restless, difficult, and dangerous. This restlessness extended across race. Even though laborers of all races shared the same plight against the Virginia gentry, and their commiserations were evident, the backlash of Bacon's Rebellion changed that. The threat to the gentry's power and authority in colonial Virginia warranted in their minds a need to redefine the class system along more rigid racial lines; this game demonstrates that process.

Bacon's Rebellion is designed to experience the making of the rebellion, to undertake military operations of the rebellion itself, and to learn about the restoration of the colony in the aftermath of the war. By the end of the game, you should have learned and be able to do the following:

1. Understand the complexity of intercultural cooperation and conflict in colonial Virginia.
2. Understand the causes of social uprisings including political exclusion, social inequality, and class conflict and racism, and apply this understanding through oral presentations, dialogues, and debates.
3. Examine and describe the beginnings of colonial transformation from a "society with slaves" to a "slave society."
4. Be able to articulate the institutionalization of American racism.
5. Demonstrate an understanding of perpetual inequality and contemporary relevance through writing.

This game takes you on a historical journey through colonial Virginia while teaching historical and civic skills including critical thinking, persuasive writing, oral articulating, and debate in an active-learning environment. Although you must adhere to the personal and factional objectives as outlined in your role sheets, you are free to defy exact history. This is not a reenactment. In playing this game, you do not reenact the history of Bacon's Rebellion, you live it.

A Note about Nomenclature

Colonial Virginia was home to several Native American groups including Pamunkeys, Doegs, Susquehannocks, and many others. Most of the European colonists were English, some born in England and some in the colony itself, and people of African descent—most of whom were enslaved, were African-born, having been captured and sold into slavery, or Virginia-born, following the status of their enslaved mothers (especially after 1662).

In this game, we have adopted the following general terminology to collectively refer to people of various racial groupings: Native Americans, Anglo-Virginians, and Afro-Virginians. In the latter two cases, we have settled on this language to use nomenclature that parallels the more commonly used Native American. "Anglo-American" is more specific than Euro-American and is used since most of the white colonists were, indeed, English. And regardless of which side of the Atlantic they were born, the term effectively captures their collective identity. Similarly, we use "Afro-Virginian" to refer to those of African descent, regardless of birthplace and regardless of whether their parentage was racially mixed (the English referred to individuals descended from both English and African as "mulatto," an archaic term that is often considered derogatory today). Those of African descent tended to share a collective sense of identity while the Anglo-Virginians who held social, economic, and political power in the colony generally recognized them as distinct from both Native Americans and the English themselves.

Used interchangeably with the term "Native Americans," "Indians," "Native people," and "Indigenous people" are also employed in game materials, consistent with current scholarly practice and generally recognized by Native American laypeople and scholars alike as acceptable and respectable terms.

For actual game play, some difficulties arise, however. Except for "Indians," the terms above are anachronistic to the time period. For example, Native people tended to use group or tribal names (such as Pamunkey) to refer to themselves. At the same time, terms used by Europeans reflected their racial assumptions, and such terms today are offensive and their use in gameplay should be avoided.

It is recommended that the GM ("game master" or "game manager") and players enter into a frank discussion of such matters early in the game setup and establish ground rules for in-game and out-of-game terminology. Since there is no escaping some anachronistic language use when twenty-first-century people inhabit roles of seventeenth-century characters, players should feel free to simply adopt in gameplay the same terms we have adopted for the game materials: Native Americans, Anglo-Virginians, and Afro-Virginians.

PROLOGUE: MY BROTHER'S KEEPER?

"For the Lord's sake shoot no more, these are our friends the Susquehannocks!" Col. George Mason yells.

You stop reloading your gun and realize what you have done. You have taken an innocent life. You were supposed to be after Doegs who had committed murderous raids along the Virginia frontier, but these are not them. These are friends. Fourteen of them have been shot down, and now one of them is on the ground, still alive, with red blood spilling out of the wound caused by the bullet from your gun. He's struggling to breathe. You bend to your knee to see if there is something that you can do, but it is too late. Choking to breathe, he looks to you, and whispers in your ear. You turn only to see his lifeless eyes staring into nothingness, frozen in time. He grabs your wrist! The grip surprises you, and the shock jolts you awake from this nightmare.

You awake in a cold sweat, but it was not just a dream, it *had* happened. The look on his dying face still haunts you weeks later. The only solace you can find is knowing that you were following orders and acting in defense of Virginia. But are these recurring nightmares a message of approaching doom?

It is just before dawn on September 11, 1675, on your farm in Westmoreland County, and since you cannot sleep anymore, you decide to get an early start on your Wednesday chores. Your tobacco plants, standing seven feet high, are ready to harvest. They must be harvested before becoming fully mature when they begin to lose value, not to mention the risk of a frost destroying the entire crop, which happened to you last harvest season. You go through the ritual in your head of cutting the plants with the knife once used by your late father. Your head is filled with memories of how he taught you to cut the tobacco—right in between the bottom leaves and the ground. The weather seems favorable today, so after cutting, you leave the tobacco on the ground for three or four hours to wilt. It has been your experience that this method results in a heavier, moister leaf, and that brings a higher profit.

You walk into the cooking area of your small farmhouse and bid good morning to your young wife who is expecting a second child. She's already up, as is her custom. You take a moment to gaze at her while she is preparing breakfast, selfishly praying that she is carrying a son. Hopefully, your service to the militia will ensure a future for your son free from Native American threats. However, a messenger arrives at the door interrupting your prayers. There have been raids on farms farther west in Stafford County, Virginia, and Charles County, Maryland. As you had expected, the fiasco the previous month alienated the Susquehannocks. You are to report at once to the docks in Jamestown to board a sloop under the command of Col. John Washington. The plan is to join Maj. Thomas Truman of Maryland in a combined campaign with Maj. Isaac Allerton's militia from Northumberland County to oust the Susquehannocks from the fort they erected near the mouth of the Piscataway Creek beside the Virginia and Maryland border. The harvest will have to wait. You eagerly join the campaign as this could ensure the security of your growing family and home.

By the time you and your fellow militiamen arrive at the fort, which is flanked by swamplands on both sides, Truman's forces have already surrounded it. Its palisade walls are made from tree trunks with gaps to allow archers to fire in defense, but no one has been able to penetrate its defenses. Since everyone in the camp seems preoccupied with their various tasks, you take the opportunity to eavesdrop on the officer's tent.

"So, my good man, what is the status?" Washington sits down to hear the report as Truman turns to him with a smirk and asks, "So, I would have thought that your governor would have sent Colonel Mason or even Colonel Brent. At least I would know that they would not shy from pulling the trigger. Nevertheless, the Susquehannocks have learned a trick or two from us, unfortunately."

"Great, first you give them arms, then you teach them to build forts?" Major Allerton provokes.

"Come now. Do not be coy, that was a different time. Besides, I was unheard of then," Truman says with a hearty laugh.

"You arrogant Marylanders!" Allerton says, keeping the mood light, and Truman returns the gesture, saying, "Well, sir, I am offended."

"It was intentional," Witty Allerton says quickly, but by this time Washington's short patience is apparent. "Well, I beg your pardon, gentlemen, but we have a task at hand, please." He insists.

Truman takes his seat at the small makeshift table and gives his report to his Virginian brothers-in-arms. "The fort is laid out in a large square with raised embankments. These embankments are on all four sides with palisades and a ditch in between. Additionally, there are bastions on each corner. It looks as though there are one hundred of their warriors guarding the fort, but it also seems as though the entire village is in there—maybe four hundred women, children, and elders. You know, they had the audacity to come out with a piece of paper and a piece of a medal that they claimed to have received from the governor of Maryland as a 'pledge of peace.' I was not convinced. They even tried to blame the Iroquois. We do not have time for this, and we do not have the artillery to batter it down. I would love to go back to my plantation and to tend to my fields, and I'm sure you would, too. We have options. We continue surrounding the fort and starve them out, but no telling when they will surrender. Or we can call a parley."

"Parley?" Allerton questions Truman.

"Yes, parley. Do I really need to give you a lesson on what a parley is?"

"Now who's being coy?" Washington chimes in. "No need for the lesson."

"Good, so we'll invite their leaders outside of the fort and charge them with the murders of our people."

"Then what?" inquires Allerton.

"We'll send them a message," Truman says. Then he notices you.

At that point you decide that it is best to be on your way. That was the last word of the conversation you hear before heeding Washington's order to join the watch.

The next day, as you head to the frontlines, news comes in that five "great men" were coming out to parley. "Finally, we can put an end to this," you think to yourself.

A message is sent all right. To your astonishment, the five emissaries lay dead, bludgeoned to death with blows to the head. One has a paper and a medal still in his hands. One still has a white flag of truce. It further shocks you that Washington, the ranking officer present, ordered the executions impatiently and wanted to capture the fort and end this standoff. You know in your heart that whatever message was intended, it was heard loud and clear, and there will be retaliation.

The "siege" drags on for another month. By this time Native Americans allied with Virginia, Piscataway warriors, and men from the Mattawan nation join the siege. Together, the Native-Anglo forces succeed in killing fifty Susquehannock warriors but fail to breach the fort's walls.

It is now November, and the militiamen are demoralized by not being able to take the fort. You overhear Colonel Washington lamenting his decision to kill the emissaries. Governor Berkeley wants Major Allerton to investigate and punish the killers, but now word comes back from Jamestown that the governor is livid. Colonel Washington confides in you that the only way to right this wrong is to take the fort and relieve Virginia of this threat to the colony's security. As he turns and looks to you with honest eyes, a messenger interrupts him, breathlessly announcing that the fort is empty! In the night, the Susquehannocks secretly escaped, killing ten men in doing so. Without blinking Washington gets ready to pursue, but you know that it will be futile.

It has been months since you have been home. Fall has turned to winter, and by now all your crops should have been harvested and stored for the cold months. As great as your loss is on your small farm, you can only imagine the loss of your superior officers who have thousands of acres and hundreds of laborers. You are almost home now, and from a distance you can see black smoke. Your heart begins to beat faster, and you enter into a gallop on your horse. Approaching your farm, you realize that it has been raided. Retaliation has come. You are enraged but more worried about your family. What happened to them? There are no human remains on the property. Your tobacco fields are burnt, your vegetable fields scorched, your house in ruins. Everyone . . . gone. What do you have left? Where is your family? Your worry turns to rage, and you head to the local burgess to get help and some answers.

In addition to being your commanding officer in the county militia, Colonel Washington is also your representative in the House of Burgesses, and it turns out that he has been called to a meeting of the Grand Assembly in Jamestown to address this issue. His servant also informs you that your farm was not the only one attacked. When asked why the governor is not doing anything about it, the servant says that he overheard a conversation between Colonel Washington and Colonel Spencer stating that Berkeley chose Sir Henry Chicheley to lead the militia against Native American raiding parties. Washington was offended by the oversight of not receiving the command but expected this treatment after his conduct at the fort, which exacerbated the conflict.

However, another servant tells you that Berkeley called off the mission in order to maintain "peaceful relations" with the Native Americans and to make sure that war and punishment is exacted on the right people. The servants share your anger—an anger that Washington could not possibly know. His farm remains intact. His lands are vast and protected while yours are vulnerable and much closer to the frontier. His family is safe and yours is gone. Why? And he's going to Jamestown to do what? Talk? You want action, you want protection, you want security. It is your right as an Englishman and as a landowner on English soil. You decide to head to Jamestown for yourself.

Before your fields were burned, you had saved up enough tobacco for a couple of weeks' stay at the Drummond Inn—it is quite pricey but worth it. There you find a temporary answer to your sorrows. You commiserate with others until you start to hear rumors about what the savages are doing to their captives. They used to assimilate them, but now they are torturing them. Your wife, daughter, and unborn child weigh heavily on your mind, troubling your sleep as your money is running out.

It is now February 1676, and you still have no word about your family. Washington has been staying at the governor's mansion near Jamestown, but what can he really do? What *would* he really do? He's not suffering like you are, and to top it off, you did not vote for him to represent you in the first place. Finally, a message from him arrives after he receives your petition for assistance on the frontier. "These are tense times, and we must handle these matters delicately. I must go, but good day to you," he writes. Not promising. You let out a loud sigh in frustration and feel a hand on your shoulder. The man introduces himself as William Drummond.

"You are the owner of this establishment?" you ask him. He laughs.

"No, that would be my wife, Sarah. Long story. What ails you?" he inquires. You tell him of your experience and the destruction of your farm.

To your surprise, he responds, "Damn that Berkeley; damn that council; damn them all! See that man sitting over there? He's new to Virginia, but he's already on the council. His name is Nathaniel Bacon and is already challenging Berkeley's actions. He just recently lost one of his servants to an Indian raid and wants revenge."

Hmmm. It seems like this Bacon could be exactly what is needed to gain control of this Indian problem once and for all. If Bacon is recruiting men to fight the invaders and secure Virginia, you want in, even if it means an open rebellion.

You see others there with the same look in their eyes as you—some of them landless, all of them tired of government inaction. You think to yourself, "The kindle is ready; Bacon's the spark."

BASIC FEATURES OF REACTING TO THE PAST

This is a historical role-playing game. Set in moments of historical tension, it places you in the role of a person from the period. By reading the game book and your individual role sheet, you will find out more about your objectives, worldview, allies, and opponents. You must then attempt to achieve victory through formal speeches, informal debate, negotiations, and conspiracy. Outcomes sometimes differ from actual history; a debriefing session sets the record straight. What follows is an outline of what you will encounter and what you will be expected to do.

Game Setup

Your instructor will spend some time before the beginning of the game helping you understand the historical context for the game. During the setup period, you will use several different kinds of material:

- The game book (what you are reading now), which includes historical information, rules and elements of the game, and essential historical documents.
- A role sheet, which provides a short biography of the historical person you will model in the game as well as that person's ideology, objectives, responsibilities, and resources. Some roles are based on historical figures.

Familiarize yourself with the documents before the game begins and return to them once you are in role. They contain information and arguments that will be useful as the game unfolds. A second reading while *in role* will deepen your understanding and alter your perspective. Once the game is in motion, your perspectives may change. Some ideas may begin to look quite different. Those who have carefully read the materials and who know the rules of the game will invariably do better than those who rely on general impressions and uncertain memories.

Game Play

Once the game begins, class sessions are run by students. In most cases, a single student serves as a sort of presiding officer. The instructor then becomes the GM and takes a seat in the back of the room. Though they do not lead the class sessions, GMs may do any of the following:

- Pass notes
- Announce important events
- Redirect proceedings that have gone off track

Instructors are, of course, available for consultations before and after game sessions. Although they will not let you in on any of the secrets of the game, they can be invaluable in terms of sharpening your arguments or finding key historical resources.

The presiding officer is expected to observe basic standards of fairness, but as a fail-safe device, most games employ the "podium rule," which allows a student who has not yet been recognized to approach the podium and wait for a chance to speak. Once at the podium, the student has the floor and must be heard.

Role sheets contain private, secret information that you must guard. Exercise caution when discussing your role with others. Your role sheet might identify likely allies, but even they may not always be trustworthy. However, keeping your own counsel and saying nothing to anyone is not an option. To achieve your objectives, you *must* speak with others. You will never muster the voting strength to prevail without allies. Collaboration and coalition building are at the heart of every game.

Some games feature strong alliances called *factions*. As a counterbalance, these games include roles called *indeterminates*. They operate outside the established factions, and while some are entirely neutral, most indeterminates possess their own idiosyncratic objectives. If you are in a faction, cultivating indeterminates is in your interest, since they can be persuaded to support your position. If you are lucky enough to have drawn the role of an indeterminate, you should be pleased; you will likely play a pivotal role in the outcome of the game.

Game Requirements

Students playing Reacting games practice persuasive writing, public speaking, critical thinking, teamwork, negotiation, problem solving, collaboration, adapting to changing circumstances, and working under pressure to meet deadlines. Your instructor will explain the specific requirements for your class. In general, though, a Reacting game asks you to perform three distinct activities:

Reading and writing. What you read can often be put to immediate use, and what you write is meant to persuade others to act the way you want them to. The reading load may vary slightly from role to role, and the writing requirement depends on your particular course. Papers are often policy statements, but they can also be autobiographies, battle plans, newspaper articles, poems, or after-game reflections. Papers often provide the foundation for the speeches delivered in class. They also help to familiarize you with the issues, which should allow you to ask good questions.

Public speaking and debate. In the course of a game, almost everyone is expected to deliver at least one formal speech from the podium (the length of the game and the size of the class will determine the number of speeches). Debate follows. It can be impromptu, raucous, and fast-paced. At some point, discussions must lead to action, which often means proposing, debating, and passing a variety of resolutions. GMs may stipulate that students deliver their papers from memory when at the podium, or they may insist that students begin to wean themselves from dependency on written notes as the game progresses.

Wherever the game imaginatively puts you, it will surely not put you in the present. Accordingly, the colloquialisms and familiarities of today's college life are out of place. Never open your speech with a salutation like "Hi guys!" when something like "Fellow citizens!" would be more appropriate.

Always seek allies to back up your points when you are speaking at the podium. Do your best to have at least one supporter second your proposal, come to your defense, or admonish inattentive members of the body. Note passing and side conversations, while common occurrences, will likely spoil the effect of your speech, so you and your supporters should insist on order before such behavior becomes too disruptive. Ask the presiding officer to assist you. Appeal to the GM as a last resort.

Strategizing. Communication among students is an essential feature of Reacting games. You will likely find yourself writing emails, texting, attending out-of-class meetings, or gathering for meals. The purpose of frequent communication is to lay out a strategy for achieving your objectives, thwarting your opponents, and hatching plots. When communicating with fellow students in or out of class, always assume that they are speaking to you in role. If you want to talk about the "real world," make that clear.

Controversy

Most Reacting games take place at moments of conflict in the past and therefore are likely to address difficult, even painful issues that we continue to grapple with today. Consequently, this game may contain controversial subject matter. You may need to represent ideas with which you personally disagree or find repugnant. When speaking about these ideas, make it clear that you are speaking *in role*. Furthermore, if other people say things that offend you, recognize that they, too, are playing roles. If you decide to respond to them, do so using the voice of your role and make this clear. If these efforts are insufficient, or the ideas associated with your particular role seem potentially overwhelming, talk to your GM.

When playing your role, rely on your role sheet and the other game materials rather than drawing on caricature or stereotype. Do not use racial and ethnic slurs even if they are historically appropriate. If you are concerned about the potential for cultural appropriation or the use of demeaning language in your game, talk to your GM.

Amid the plotting, debating, and voting, always remember that this is an immersive role-playing game. Other players may resist your efforts, attack your ideas, and even betray a confidence. They take these actions because they are playing their roles. If you become concerned about the potential for game-based conflict to bleed out into the real world, take a step back and reflect on the situation. If your concerns persist, talk to your GM.

2

Historical Background

CHRONOLOGY

1607	Virginia Company of London founds Jamestown, the first permanent English settlement in North America
1610–11	The "Starving Time"
1610–14	The First Anglo-Powhatan War; John Rolfe and Pocahontas marry, contributing to the new Anglo-Native peace
1617	First shipment of tobacco to England
1619	Headright system established; Virginia House of Burgesses established; twenty enslaved Africans arrive in Jamestown
1622–32	The Second Anglo-Powhatan War
1624	King James I revokes Virginia Company's charter, making it a royal colony
1641	Sir William Berkeley appointed as governor of Virginia
1644–46	The Third Anglo-Powhatan War
1652	Berkeley removed as governor during the English Civil War due to his support for Charles I
1660	The Crown is restored in England, and Charles II returns Berkeley to the governorship
1674	Nathaniel Bacon settles at the Curles Neck Plantation in Henrico County
March 3, 1675	Governor Berkeley appoints Bacon to the council of state
July 1675	In the Northern Neck, Doeg Indians steal hogs from planter Thomas Mathew because he failed to pay them for their trade goods. Colonists kill several Indians, and in retaliation, the Doeg kill his herdsman, Robert Hen.
August 1675	Colonial expedition against the Doeg Indians in Maryland indiscriminately kills

several Susquehannocks, allies of the English.

Late August 1675
News of settler-Indian war in New England arrives in Virginia

September 1675
Isaac Allerton Jr. and John Washington, commissioned by Governor Berkeley to investigate matters on the Virginia-Maryland border, instead kill several Susquehannock emissaries and besiege 500 of them in their fort on the upper Potomac River.

November 1675
The Susquehannocks break the siege and escape to the piedmont region.

December 1675
The Susquehannocks settle their civilians in several winter camps spread across the piedmont from the Roanoke River to the James River.

January 1676
Susquehannock warriors launch a series of retributive attacks on Virginian settlements along the upper Rappahannock River and attack several more near the James River falls, including Bacon's Quarter, Nathaniel Bacon's secondary plantation.

Late January 1676
Governor Berkeley commissions Sir Henry Chicheley to lead an expedition against the Susquehannocks but inexplicably cancels the order before the 300-man battalion can depart.

March 1676
"The Long Assembly" convenes: the council of state and the House of Burgesses meet in joint session to address the Indian crisis.

"MOST EXCELLENT FRUITS": A HISTORICAL OVERVIEW OF COLONIAL VIRGINIA TO 1676

Introduction

Virginia's history starts not with the founding of Jamestown, but with the Indigenous people who long preceded the English as rightful occupants of the land. The most significant of these were the Powhatan, members of the most populous Native American linguistic group, the Algonquians. Algonquian speakers could be found from the east coast of North America to the Rocky Mountains, and the members of their tribes numbered in the hundreds of thousands (today, Algonquian speakers live throughout the United States and Canada). The Eastern Algonquians included many of the tribes who felt the first brunt of European colonialism: the Massachusett, Narragansett, Mohegan, Lenape, Piscataway, Nanticoke, among many others. But it was the Powhatan peoples who dominated eastern Virginia and western Maryland calling the region Tsenacommacah or "densely inhabited land."

By the early seventeenth century, Wahunsenacawh, a Powhatan *weronance* or chief, came to lead a confederacy of thirty Powhatan tribes. As a Mamanatowick or paramount chief, Wahunsenacawh oversaw 15,000 people at the height of the confederacy's power and influence; it covered 6,000 square miles, much of it ignorantly claimed by England as the colony of Virginia. The Powhatan Confederacy was just that—a confederation of groups and villages with distinct but small-scale polities (compared to European nation-states), and each associated with distinct territories. This was not an empire nor a sharply hierarchical society. The constituent groups maintained ties with one another through ritual gift giving and other social-based diplomatic protocols. Furthermore, Native leaders earned respect through seniority, military prowess, and the ability to give gifts rather than commanding deference through the assertion of power and authority. Wahunsenacawh was apparently deeply respected and therefore had

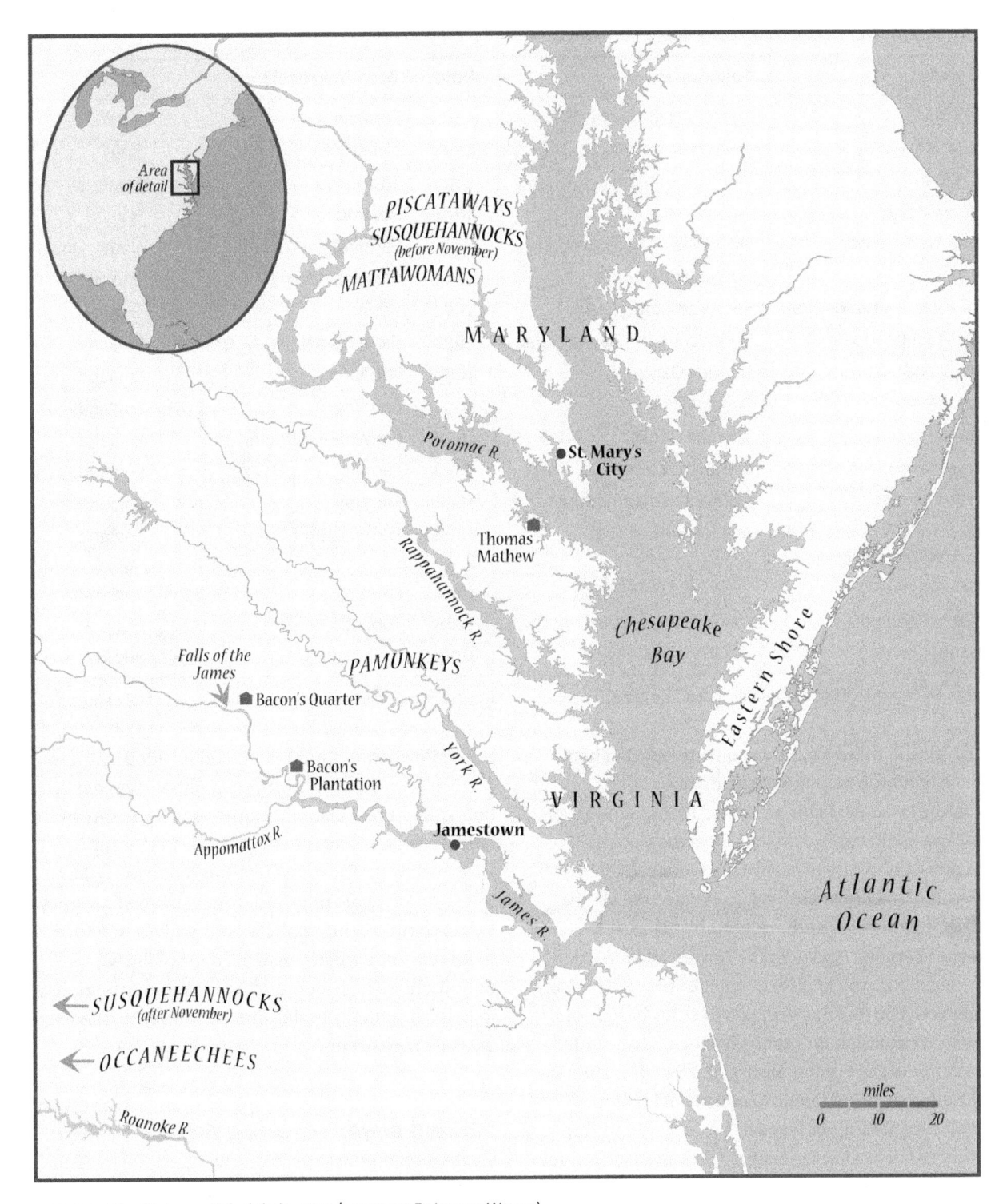

MAP 2.1 The Colony of Virginia in 1675 (courtesy Rebecca Wrenn)

TABLE 2.1 North American colonies, 1565–1670

Colony	Founder(s)	Date	Economic basis	Nation
Florida	Pedro Menendez de Aviles	1565	Farming	Spain
New Mexico	Juan de Onate	1598	Livestock	Spain
Virginia	Virginia Company	1607	Tobacco	England
New France	France	1608	Fur trading	France
New Netherland	Dutch West India Company	1621	Farming, fur trading	Netherlands
Plymouth	Puritan separatists	1620	Farming, fishing	England
St. Kitts, Barbados et al.	European immigrants	1624	Sugar	England
Massachusetts Bay	Massachusetts Bay Company	1630	Farming, fishing, fur trading	England
Maryland	Cecilius Calvert	1634	Tobacco	England
Rhode Island	Roger Williams	1636	Farming	England
Connecticut	Thomas Hooker	1636	Farming, fur trading	England
New Haven	Massachusetts migrants	1638	Farming	England
New Hampshire	Massachusetts migrants	1638	Farming	England
New York (formerly New Netherland)	James, duke of York	1664	Farming, fur trading	England
New Jersey	John Lord Berkeley	1664	Farming	England
North Carolina	Carolina proprietors	1665	Tobacco, forest products	England
South Carolina	Carolina proprietors	1670	Rice, Indigo	England

Note: By 1670, England's dominance over the Atlantic seaboard of North America was evident, and Virginia was at its center.

significant influence over a confederacy that had developed substantial intergroup ties.

Long before the English settled in the Chesapeake region, Spain created an empire in the wealthiest regions in the Americas. But the French, Dutch, Swedes, and the English all challenged the claims of the Spanish in North America by the early seventeenth century. Although the slowest at overseas colonization, the English eventually proved the most aggressive in forming expansive settler-based colonies compared to the relatively more lightly settled colonies of the French, Dutch, and Swedes. Through the efforts of the Virginia Company of London, Jamestown, Virginia, was settled, followed by the work of other companies and the creation of several other settlements throughout the seventeenth century. Between 1607 and 1700 more than a half a million people left England; the majority of these settled in North America.

The Powhatans found their land invaded by these English settlers, and the eventual impact was devastating. But it was not only immigrants from England who wrought changes to their lands. Beginning in 1619, enslaved Africans were imported to the colony. These unfortunate men and women shaped colonial Virginia while being exploited themselves. Virginia, in fact, became a place of racial oppression where both Indigenous people and Africans became subject to English settler colonialism while never surrendering their own agency.

"Great & Ample": Creating Virginia

Virginia's founding as a colony was inspired by Richard Hakluyt, England's leading publicist for overseas expansion, who proclaimed in 1599: "There is under our noses the great & ample countery of Virginia." On paper, the territory claimed by the English as Virginia stretched from modern-day Vermont to North Carolina and promised "the most excellent fruits." But it remained nothing more than an unrealized dream until the Virginia Company of London was authorized by King James I to colonize the Chesapeake Bay. Even after the first 105 Englishmen landed in 1607 and named their new settlement—and the river it was founded on—after the king, material success would be long in coming.

Their hopes of immediate rewards were quickly disappointed, as the gold and precious gems Hakluyt dreamed of were nowhere to be found in the marshy lands of Virginia. Jamestown soon entered a "starving time" as the ill-equipped colonists could neither grow their own food nor maintain stable peaceful relations with the Indians. They resorted to scavenging for berries and bark, boiling shoe leather to eat, and even cannibalism. In fact, one settler was executed for this desperate act. And they also suffered from sickness and disease. The death toll was catastrophic as colonists were reduced from 500 to 60. But a ship arrived with fresh colonists and supplies in the summer of 1610, just as the remaining settlers were heading for home. Restocked and rejuvenated, the English colonists committed to making another go of it.

But while even survival was a struggle in the earliest years, the colony eventually found its raison d'être through English taste for Orinoco tobacco. John Rolfe, an English merchant and early resident of the colony, correctly predicted that West Indian tobacco—spreading in popularity in England—could flourish in Virginia soil and introduced it in 1612. With a viable staple crop, plentiful land, and European demand for their product, early settlers reaped handsomely from the seeds they sowed. Their only limitation was in labor, which was scarce and costly.

Tobacco transformed Virginia in innumerable ways but had its greatest impact on those who were easily oppressed—Native Americans, Africans, and poor Englishmen. As a repetitious, time-consuming, and labor-intensive task, growing tobacco involved cultivating, harvesting, curing, and transporting the crops, requiring a strong and reliable workforce. The first source of labor was indentured servants from England. Beginning in 1619, labor migration from England was stimulated through the headright system, which took advantage of plentiful and cheap land, at least in the minds of Virginia Company directors who failed to recognize Native land claims or political sovereignty. Consequently, they offered fifty acres of land and free transport to each person willing to indenture themselves as servants for four to seven years in the colony. A person who paid his own or a family member's passage also earned a headright of fifty acres for each. This also applied to payment of passage for any laborer. In other words, a planter in the Chesapeake could simultaneously obtain land and labor by importing workers from England. Profits could then be invested in importing more indentured servants in order to gain more land. Indentured servants accounted for 75–85 percent of the immigrants to Virginia. But they were not the only source of labor; as outlined below, both Native Americans and, especially, Africans involuntarily supplied labor for the colony.

Soon a planter gentry began to form, and upward social mobility depended upon control of servants, land, and tobacco profits. Opportunities for advancement—for those who managed to survive—were real. Former servants could become independent farmers, that is, "freeholders," and live a comfortable lifestyle. Some even assumed positions of political prominence such as county militia officer or justice of the peace; similar achievements in England were highly unlikely.

Because tobacco planting depleted the soil, new land was essential for sustaining and expanding plant yields. Mother nature wrought devastating results as well from storms to droughts. And there was the ongoing threat of Native American hostilities.

"Our Late Reconsiled Salvage Enymies": Anglo–Native American Relations in Colonial Virginia

When the English established themselves at James Fort in 1607, Wahunsenacawh, known by the English as "Chief Powhatan," sent an ambassador to seek peace and promised a delivery of food following the Native harvest. This auspicious beginning to Anglo-Indian relations was short-lived. Relations waxed and waned and two wars broke out in the first fifteen years of the colony's life. The 1622 council of state report on the second war revealed the deteriorating English attitudes toward the Indians in making reference to their "late reconsiled salvage enymies." Indeed, the conflict would not end until the Powhatan Confederacy had effectively disintegrated, the Indian population was decimated by disease and warfare, they had lost most of their land, and they had become politically dependent upon the Virginians.

Native American-European relations took place in a context of conflicting worldviews. Among the many differences were those rooted in assumptions about cultural superiority and political sovereignty. The Powhatan people were mystified by Europeans who had access to novel technology but apparently could not meet their own basic need to feed themselves. Meanwhile, they naturally saw them as (at best) interlopers in their sovereign territory or (at worst) invaders. For their part, the English explored North America and established colonies with a profound sense of cultural superiority. By the right of discovery, as the English asserted, they claimed huge swaths of North America over the claims of other Europeans. Native claims were tolerated as a practical matter, but since the English saw Indians to be lacking in civilization, they presumed they had no natural claim to the land. Out of such competing assumptions came a cycle of agreements, conflict, war, and rapprochements. But with each cycle, the Powhatans lost land and sovereignty by degrees.

The history of the earliest encounters between the English and Powhatans are wrapped up in the legends spawned by John Smith's self-promoting and imaginative writing. Was he captured by the Powhatans? Rescued by Pocahontas? Scholars continue to debate these details and the nuances of the encounter as he reported them. But there seems to have been an early agreement that in exchange for food, the colonists would supply the Powhatans with weapons and open trade. The English staged an elaborate ceremony granting a copper crown and a scarlet cloak to the Powhatan chief.

However, within a couple of years, the colonists began to expand their settlement outside of the fort, and this disrupted the arrangement. The English did not truly respect Native political sovereignty, and Algonquian and English concepts of property ownership significantly differed, a difference that led to much bloodshed. Most Powhatan villages held their land communally, such that individual plots of land could not be bought or sold. Meanwhile, English livestock, left free to forage in the countryside, seemed no different to the Indians than the wildlife they hunted for food. As colonists settled and took possession of land instead of just erecting trading posts, and Native Americans helped themselves to the bounty of land as they always had (including free-range livestock), conflict and battles over territory were inevitable. But the Anglo-Powhatan Wars were not just minor conflicts over land and property. They were deadly wars of conquest and self-preservation.

First Anglo-Powhatan War, 1610–1614

Beginning in August 1610, the English, under the command of Lord De La Warr, burned the nearest Powhatan villages in suspicion that they were harboring runaway colonists, destroying much needed corn in the process. Widespread conflict ensued. It was rumored that one Powhatan woman elder, taken captive, was forced to watch as English colonists threw her children in the river and shot them in their heads before stabbing her to death. Native people were forced to abandon their villages, and many never returned. By 1611, both sides experienced heavy losses, but the English made steady expansion into Powhatan territory as Wahunsenacawh began to lose authority over the confederacy. When the

English kidnapped Pocahontas in the winter of 1612, a cease-fire temporarily ensued. Although sporadic fighting continued for nearly a year, the end came when Sir Thomas Dale launched an attack, Pocahontas in tow, on Wahunsenacawh's new capital in March 1614. Peace on both sides was sought in part through the marriage of Pocahontas to John Rolfe, an option the English considered acceptable because of her conversion to Christianity.

Their union initiated a brief period of peace but was cut short by her death in 1616 while traveling with her husband and infant son in England. Tensions further escalated upon Wahunsenacawh's death in 1618, which brought his younger brother, Opechanacanough, to power. The new leader faced increased English immigration which in turn led to increased conflict.

Second Anglo-Powhatan War, 1622–1632

On March 22, 1622, Chief Opechanacanough renewed Powhatan resistance to the English invasion, making a series of surprise attacks on colonial settlements. The murder of his advisor, Nemattanew, was the motivating factor. They raided over thirty settlements and plantations, mostly in outlying areas, killing about a third of the English population. Ostensibly, Jamestown survived because a converted Native American named Chauco alerted the settlement, although some scholars argue that Opechanacanough intentionally spared Jamestown, only wanting to force the English back to their original settlement. More than 400 colonists lost their lives and twenty women were taken captive.

But the English did not take the hint and, allied with the Accomac and Patawomeck, undertook a brutal counteroffensive. Historian William S. Powell described the devastating effects of the English total warfare policy on the Indians: "The use of force, surprise attacks, famine resulting from the burning of their corn, destroying their boats, canoes, and houses, breaking their fishing weirs and assaulting them in their hunting expeditions, pursuing them with horses and using bloodhounds to find them and mastiffs to 'seaze' them, driving them as they fled into the hands of their enemies among other tribes, and 'animating and abetting their enemies against them.'"[1]

Opechanacanough decided to negotiate in a peace parley in 1623, but leaders from Jamestown arrived with poisoned liquor for the ceremonial toast and killed over 200 of them. Chief Opechanacanough escaped unharmed, and war continued intermittently for several years with the English generally maintaining the upper hand. It was not until September 30, 1632, that the two sides reached a peace agreement.

Meanwhile, the colonists continued to expand, both during and after the war, settling on both sides of the James River and across the Chesapeake Bay on the Eastern Shore. They also moved across the Virginia Peninsula (bordered by the James River to the south and the York River to the north) and began settling along both sides of the York River. They built a palisade across the Virginia Peninsula in order to exclude Native people and to protect their free-ranging cattle.

Third Anglo-Powhatan War, 1644–1646

By 1664, the pressures of English settler colonialism on the Powhatan people again became too much to bear, and Opechanacanough, now in his late eighties by some estimates, rallied the remnants of the Powhatan Confederacy and attacked the colony on March 18. Some 400 settlers lost their lives, reducing Virginia's ever-growing population by only 10 percent. While not insignificant, these casualties amounted to a much smaller portion of the colonial population than the 1622 attack. Nevertheless, in the eyes of the English, it was too much bloodshed, and the threat had to be eliminated. By July, Virginians marched against the main tribes of the Powhatan Confederacy: the Appomattoc, Weyanoke, Warraskoyak, Nansemond, Chowanoke, and Secotan. After constructing forts at the fall line of each of the major rivers, the governor himself led a march to storm Opechanacanough's stronghold, successfully capturing and bringing him back to Jamestown where he was assassinated by a guard. His death ended the

Powhatan Confederacy. In October 1646, England entered into a treaty with the former constituent members of the confederacy, each tribe becoming tributaries to the English Crown.

The end of the Third Anglo-Powhatan War represented the beginning of thirty years of relative peace between the Virginians and their Algonquian neighbors, although it was hardly more than military subjection. Relieved from the threat of ongoing Indian attacks, the colonists, especially recent immigrants, focused on enlarging their landholdings. But as new settlers pushed into Virginia's backcountry, the potential for violence with distant Native groups increased. Meanwhile, a system of trade developed between English traders and both local and distant Native people that included the exchange of food items, animal skins and furs, and, eventually, slaves, consisting of Indians captured in war and sold to the English.

"Masterless Men": Creating Anglo-Virginians

Virginia presented unique opportunities to Englishmen who valued land ownership above all else. In sixteenth- and seventeenth-century England, "working for wages was itself widely associated with servility and the loss of liberty." According to historian Eric Foner, "Only those who controlled their own labor could be regarded as truly free."[2] Indeed, in English law, only those who owned land could vote.

Because Virginia appeared to present an unlimited bounty of free land, it became synonymous with the opportunity to achieve freedom. Englishmen came to Virginia to gain or regain economic independence through land acquisition and profit making through tobacco production. The possibility of passing property on to heirs was also attractive.

In addition to economic independence, land ownership in Virginia granted the right to vote; those with this right were known as "freeholders." These ranged from the gentry—larger landowners with thousands of acres and hundreds of servants—to yeoman farmers—small landowners with no servants. But freeholding status was not available to everyone. Generally speaking, only men could own property, and only white men could vote. But for these white men, Virginia offered the opportunity to rise rapidly in social position in ways that were impossible in England.

After 1619, the company sought to further entice mostly young, untitled men from farming and laboring families in England to immigrate to Virginia with promises of English freedoms such as the right to trial by jury and a representative form of government. From 1607 to the end of the 1640s, the lure of property and expanded political rights led over 6,000 English colonists to immigrate to Virginia. In population, the English colonies saw more immigration to its colonies than its European rivals. Some thrived, others went back home, but most died. Virginia in the 1640s offered quick wealth and social mobility to only a few. The majority of colonists who survived and actually came to own land possessed small holdings of fifty to a few hundred acres.

The Virginia colonists worked hard clearing forests for their crops as demand for tobacco increased. Virginia's exports rose from a total weight of 2,000 pounds in 1615 to 500,000 in 1626. By 1640, almost 1.4 million pounds of tobacco were shipped annually to London, and even with low prices, Virginia managed to profit greatly from this "most excellent fruit."

But tobacco was a labor-intensive crop, and success depended upon the growth of a plantation system largely reliant on a labor force of English servants and some enslaved Africans. Along with the growth of tobacco and the evolution of the plantation system came a growing mass of working poor.

Many families grew in wealth and power, since social and economic advance created access to political position, which in turn aided and abetted the increase of wealth. Headrights became an expression of patronage, and colonial governors favored their supporters with headright grants and servants. Additional patronage came through the distribution of political office—everything from serving on the council of state to holding local (county) office.

Beneath the freeholders on Virginia's socio-economic ladder stood white laborers, or freemen: landless poor young men who were either unemployed or who worked as apprentices, overseers, or at other skilled or unskilled labor. Laborers were typically former indentured servants who did not obtain land upon the end of their term and subsisted as wage laborers. Unlike their landowning counterparts, they did not have the right to vote. This had not always been the case, however. For a time in Virginia's history, all white freemen could vote; but legislation passed in 1670 limited suffrage to freeholders.

Indentured Servants

Most white Virginians arrived in the colony as indentured servants. An indenture was a contract in which men or women agreed to work as servants in exchange for transportation to Virginia and some supplies and provisions known as "freedom dues" to be given after their time of service. They came from many walks of life in England, and upon signing up to serve, had little control over their destination—whether the West Indies or the Chesapeake Bay. Adults ostensibly served for four to seven years and children sometimes much longer; most worked in the colony's tobacco fields owned by planters. Terms could be extended if the indenture was violated in any way. Servants were particularly at risk of premature death—it is estimated that five of every six servants did not survive their indentures in the first thirty years of the colony's history. Some 100,000 died during this period.

Those who survived and completed their term of service became "freedmen" and often sought to establish themselves as farmers or planters in their own right. Such opportunities were greater in the earliest decades of the seventeenth century. But after the midpoint, the only land available to newly freed men was in the hinterlands. Settling the backcountry tended to yield more risk than profits. The farther one settled from the navigable rivers, the less access to transportation and the greater the threat of conflict with Native Americans.

Women in Colonial Virginia

Women played a key role in colonial Virginia and faced both special challenges and unique opportunities. Like men, indentured women saw "a life of hard labor in the tobacco fields and early death."[3] As with women in England, they possessed few rights as individuals. Many indentures for women prohibited marriage, and becoming pregnant put them at risk of term extension.

However, because of the demand for male labor in tobacco fields, women numbered only one to every four or five men in the colony, giving them a different kind of value and in turn a certain empowerment. Their terms were often bought out by single or widowed men of means who sought marriage partners.

Meanwhile, Virginia continued to have relatively high mortality rates, and women who survived their husbands soon found themselves courted by unattached males. With each marriage opportunity came the likelihood of social advancement. Consider, for example, the case of Elizabeth Willoughby, daughter of Thomas Willoughby II. She was first married to Dutch merchant Simon Overzee, who died in 1660 or before. She then married the London merchant George Colclough. Unfortunately, this marriage was short-lived, for records in 1662 demonstrate that Elizabeth had again been widowed and was then married to Issac Allerton, a merchant of New England. All three husbands were residents of Virginia.

But any inheritances due Elizabeth became the property of her successive husbands, which was basically true for all women in Virginia. Elizabeth's own mother, Sarah Tompson, was coheir with her sister when their father died, but court records (see the relevant core text below) show that her inheritance passed to her husband, Thomas Willoughby II. However, because of the social instability wrought by frequent deaths in Virginia, widows could effectively gain the right to own property when they inherited land through their husbands' estates, especially in the absence of husbands and male heirs. This significantly contrasted with the situation in England where women rarely held property in their own name and generally had no individual standing before the law. But while women could work their way up through the social ranks in Virginia, young men had fewer avenues for social and economic advancement open to them.

"20 and Odd Negroes": Creating Afro-Virginians

Especially after the English defeated the Powhatans, freeholders still depended primarily on English laborers, but more tobacco planters began to import small numbers of enslaved Africans as well. The first had arrived in the colony in 1619. Historian Ira Berlin called them "Atlantic Creoles," highlighting their presence and significance but also noting that slavery did not dominate colonial Virginia society in the seventeenth century. It was but one of several coexisting labor systems. In other words, early colonial Virginia was a "society with slaves" and not a "slave society." Nevertheless, the Africans who were forced to migrate to the colony developed into a community of Afro-Virginians while also integrating into the larger colonial society in various ways.[4]

In 1619, a Portuguese slaver called the *Sao Joao Bautista* captained by Manuel Mendes da Cunha purchased 300 enslaved Angolans with intentions of selling them in the Spanish colonies. They were from Luanda, the recently established capital of the Portuguese colony of Angola. At the time, King Alvaro III Nimi a Mpanzu, *manikongo* (king) of the Kingdom of Kongo just north of Angola, was actively involved in the transatlantic slave trade, and Portugal had been exporting enslaved West Africans from there for hundreds of years. The *Sao Joao Bautista* was captured by two ships sailing under Dutch letters of marque. One of these, the *White Lion*, made for Jamestown in order to reprovision and to sell the slaves taken as their portion of the *Bautista* booty.

John Rolfe himself logged the historic Jamestown exchange in a 1620 letter, recalling that "he [Dutch Captain Jope] brought not any thing but 20. and odd Negroes, which the Governor and Cape Marchant bought for victuals (whereof he was in greate need as he pretended) at the best and easyest rate they could."[5]

Slaves or Servants?

It is sometimes claimed that because the English colony did not have a system of slavery (that is, a set of laws and customary practices regarding slavery) in place prior to the arrival of these enslaved Africans, the Virginians treated them as servants with limited terms rather than slaves. It is further assumed that as servants, they had the same opportunities as English servants to become landowners after becoming freemen. Along with such claims, it is asserted that racist attitudes that may have existed among the English did not prevent people of African descent from advancing their interests or gaining their freedom. In contrast, some people are of the opinion that racism and race-based slavery always went hand in hand and manifested themselves in the same debasing and exploitative ways.

On the one hand, it *is* true that some individuals of African descent were recorded in Virginia court records as plaintiffs or defendants, and some even won cases against Englishmen in disputes over property, debt, and their freedom. In such cases, there was a form of racial equality. On the other hand, the first twenty Angolans to arrive in the colony were enslaved and not indentured. Some may have served limited terms, but their terms were longer than those typically served by the English and, more importantly, were involuntary. Africans may have worked side by side with English servants in the tobacco fields, but they knew full well that a color line limited their advancement. In a few notable cases, some individuals crossed that line, improving their social status and challenging European dominance, but these were rare exceptions to an increasingly rigid rule.

Thus, slavery did exist and was expanding in Virginia, albeit slowly. Through the 1680s, the number of white indentured servants outnumbered enslaved Africans, roughly at a rate of two to one, but likely in even higher ratios during some early decades (in 1671, Governor Berkeley estimated that the population of Virginia was "above forty thousand persons, men, women and children, ... of which there are two thousand black slaves [and] six thousand Christian servants"). Over the years, however, unfortunate Africans continued to be brought to the colony under duress to serve as slaves. If not formally considered slaves for life, their terms were of indefinite length or for such periods (for example, ninety-nine years) that were effectively life terms.

Native Americans were also pressed into service, some being referred to as "slaves" even before Africans arrived in the colony. In each of the Anglo-Indian wars, Native captives were enslaved. After the third war, the colonial traders actively exchanged goods with neighboring tribes in exchange for captive Indians destined for slavery. Some Native people —often children—served as slaves on Virginian plantations while others were exported for servitude elsewhere.

Cost and availability limited the number of African slaves, but they did enter the colony throughout the seventeenth century. And while they comprised a small number of the bonded labor (along with indentured English servants and enslaved Indians), their labor was monopolized by elite planters who could afford the higher cost of long-term laborers. Enslaved Africans were the preferred form of labor, a preference rooted in the intersection of economic interest and racist sentiments that laid the foundation for race-based slavery.

The Case of Anthony Johnson and the Limits of Freedom and Opportunity for Afro-Virginians

But as noted before, there existed exceptions to the rule of keeping people of color enslaved. One such Afro-Virginian was Anthony Johnson. Born in Africa, presumably Angola, Johnson arrived at Jamestown in 1621 and escaped the Native American attacks in following years to serve out a term of service after which his master, John Littleton, released him. By 1652, he received 250 acres in land through the headright system after importing five servants, some of them English. Even his sons, John and Richard, accumulated land through the headright system. Though not a part of the elite planter class, his 1654 lawsuit against his slave, John Casor, and his neighbor, Mr. Parker, was successful, awarding him Casor's service for life. Parker was also ordered to pay the court fees. Thus, Johnson proved his rights as a Virginian slave owner and landowner. Eventually, the Johnson clan would sell their holdings in Virginia and establish residence in Maryland, taking John Casor with them.

It might be assumed that Johnson's victory and the success of those of similar status and experience are proof of racial equality in early colonial Virginia; however, while it is true that a few industrious individuals with the support of powerful patrons did achieve significant economic and social status, Afro-Virginians were never truly equal and did not share the same opportunities as free whites. Johnson, for example, though a landowner, was not a freeholder and did not vote, a crucial point of distinction in English society. He also could not be elected or serve in government due to the simple fact that he was not English. He was a part of a very small population of free Afro-Virginians who found opportunities for self-advancement in a colonial society still in its infancy.

Anti-African sentiment existed well before the arrival of the first Blacks in the colony and persisted as the presence of people of color increased. And as Anglo-Virginians perceived a threat to their established authority, courts in Virginia began to dispense more racially discriminatory justice. This is amply demonstrated from a 1640 court case in which punishment was racially administered to three runaway servants. The two English servants were ordered to serve just an additional year each, but the African-born servant was forced to serve for the rest of his life.

Virginia Statutes Concerning Race

Indeed, the legislative record in Virginia demonstrates a steady restriction on the rights of Africans while at the same time expanding the rights of Englishmen and those who claimed ownership of Afro-Virginians (see table 2.2). Perhaps the most promi-

TABLE 2.2 Virginia statutes concerning race, 1630–1672

Year	Statute
1639–40	An act demanding all persons except those of African descent to provide themselves with arms and ammunition or be fined at the discretion of the governor and council.
1642–43	An act creating the first legal distinction between English and African women.
1644–45	An act counting African women and their descendants among the tithes.
1660–61	An act punishing English servants running away with those of African descent.
March 1661–62	An act discouraging white indentured servants from running away with enslaved people.
March 1661–62	An act prohibiting trading among indentured servants and enslaved people.
December 1662	An act applying the free status of the mother on children.
1667	An act declaring that baptism does not alter the status of enslaved people.
1668	An act declaring that women of African descent are taxable.
1669	An act legalizing the punishment and killing of enslaved people.
October 1670	An act prohibiting free people of color and Native Americans from owning white servants.
October 1670	An act creating additional distinction between Black people and Native Americans.
September 1672	An act requiring all enslaved children to be registered for tithes.
September 1672	An act to suppress the rebellious activities of enslaved people.

Note: This summary of laws demonstrates that even though English settlers were racially conscious, they did not have an established system of laws to distinguish between individuals of English and African descent. Instead, the laws evolved over the colonies' history as a perceived need to limit the rights and responsibilities of Africans in favor of the English.

nent and pernicious of these was the 1662 law that determined a child's legal status should follow that of the mother and not the father, which directly contravened English law.

One need not look far for the rationale behind this law. African women were valued for their labor but also for their childbearing attributes. This doomed all children of enslaved mothers to a lifetime of slavery, regardless of their father's status. It also created a perpetual population of slaves.

Many of Virginia's laws establishing race-based slavery did so without mentioning race, but this was hardly accidental. For example, in 1670, the colonial assembly passed a law that declared "all servants not being christians imported into this colony by shipping shalbe slaves for their lives." The non-Christian designation effectively excluded an English servant, and while it was possible that some enslaved Africans had become Christians after arriving in the colony, a 1667 law made clear that "the conferring of baptisme doth not alter the condition of the person as to his bondage or freedome."[6]

Race and Racism in Seventeenth-Century Virginia

It is important to recognize that English concepts of race and expressions of racism were nuanced and evolving. English notions of their superiority over others were cultural as well as racial. Associating civilization with religion (Christianity), with European forms of agriculture, and with their own political institutions, the English saw themselves as superior to both Native Americans and Africans. But their attitudes toward Indians could vary considerably from those they held regarding Africans. Part of the English rationale saw Native Americans as only lacking in civilization, and therefore they might rise above their natural state through education and evangelism. But the English also tended to categorize Indians as "good" (that is, friendly to the English) and "bad" (enemies who were considered savage and unredeemable). Furthermore, Native resistance to civilization—obstinate adherence to their own "savagery" by not adopting or exhibiting English cultural practices—sometimes led the English to consider Native Americans as expendable obstacles to English civilization and expansion.

Meanwhile, despite the presence of Africans who adopted Christianity and English economic and social practices, emerging ideas about the racial inferiority of people with "black" skin was reinforced by the degrading effects of brutal enslavement. The English, therefore, increasingly justified slavery of Africans due to their race even as their belief in African racial inferiority was undergirded by the very status of slavery imposed upon them. Slavery itself was justified by the English on the grounds that those enslaved were not Christians and had been taken as captives in war—two long-standing ideas associated with slavery among Europeans. This was coupled with the dubious biblical interpretation that Africans were descendants of Noah's son, Ham, whose descendants were cursed to serve the descendants of his brothers, Shem and Japheth. This mythology contributed to racist assumptions about Africans, while at the same time it was not applicable to Native Americans who presumably were not Ham's descendants. Moreover, the taint of Ham's blood was sufficient to categorize an individual as nonwhite. The English recognized those of mixed ancestry with the term "mulatto," which technically meant having one white and one Black parent. Practically speaking, however, the English saw anyone with Black ancestry as mulatto and therefore inferior to whites.

"The Governor, Council and Assembly": Government and Politics

From 1619 on, English colonists enjoyed representative government in Virginia and the protection of English freedoms, such as the right to trial by jury and to form a representative government. This was in an effort to encourage settlers to come to Virginia. The colonial government consisted of a governor, governor's council, and a legislative assembly that first met on July 30, 1619, and which became known as the House of Burgesses in 1642. The burgesses, twenty-two elected representatives, first convened in the church in Jamestown. The governor and the council of state were originally appointed by the Virginia Company.

Although the colony began under the auspices of the Virginia Company of London, King Charles I assumed control in 1624 after ongoing Indian troubles. From that point on, the Crown appointed the governor, and the elite of the colony became an extension of the king's patronage. But the basic structure of the government remained the same throughout the seventeenth century. When reporting on the state of the colony in 1671 and answering the query "Where are the legislative and executive powers of your government seated?" Governor Berkeley simply answered, "In the governor, council and assembly, and officers substituted by them."

Voting was commonplace and a long-standing tradition in both Virginia and in England. The House of Burgesses was the first representative assembly in English America, but it derived from English practice. Unlike England, however, property qualifications were not required for white men to vote before 1670, creating a potentially genuine democratic place. Even after that time, the proportion of white men

TABLE 2.3 Tudor and Stuart monarchs of England, 1558–1685

Monarch	Reign	Relation to predecessor
Elizabeth I	1558–1603	Half sister to Mary I
James I	1603–25	Cousin
Charles I	1625–49 (executed)	Son
Charles II	1660–85	Son

who could vote was greater in Virginia than in England because property ownership, while limited, was still more widespread than in the motherland.

Through the right to vote, white Virginians could elect representatives to the House of Burgesses—two burgesses per county—with whom rested the power to levy taxes and pass other legislation for the colony. It is also true, however, that all laws had to be approved by the governor and his council. Meanwhile, all women, men of color, and whites who did not own land had no direct say in government. (It was presumed that all were represented through fathers, husbands, or masters, insofar as it was believed at the time that they deserved or needed representation at all.)

And while any adult white male meeting the property qualifications could vote and therefore hold office, only the most well established could afford the time to serve as a burgess. Even though the assembly did not conduct a significant amount of business, they approached that business in a leisurely fashion. Legislative sessions would last for weeks, if not months, and the average person had little time to spare for such protracted gatherings. Attending to one's farm or trade or business preoccupied most men otherwise qualified to serve. The elite, however, with their vast labor supply, were readily able to hold such offices.

The influence of the electorate was further reduced through low voter turnout. Virginia's population was widely dispersed, with few settlements and most settlers living on scattered farms and plantations. Thus, participating in elections entailed time-consuming long-distance travel. Elected burgesses owed their offices to a few voting freeholders. Effectively, burgesses represented the needs of only a few rather than the needs of all in their districts.

The Berkeley Administration

Many men served at the king's pleasure in the role of governor, but none equaled in prestige or impact to Sir William Berkeley. Scion of a family favored in the court of England's Charles I, he was appointed governor of Virginia in 1641 and served the better part of the next three decades. Berkeley's character was marked by a profound commitment to the Crown but also a deep investment in the colony. Not long after arriving in the colony, he built Green Spring mansion, establishing his long-term commitment to the colony and elite society there. His dual commitment was also represented by his voyages back to England on behalf of the colony and his support for the Crown during England's civil wars.

In the final effort by the Powhatans to resist the English invasion of their homelands, Berkeley led troops into the field himself, finally subjecting the confederacy. From that point forward, he managed a successful Native diplomatic agenda, not only preventing further attacks by former members of the Powhatan Confederacy but also enlisting them in defense of the colony against outlying tribes.

Although Berkeley was well liked by the Virginians he ruled, events in England led to his removal from office in the 1650s. Both in England and in Virginia, Berkeley remained loyal to the Crown. In fact, when word arrived in Virginia of the beheading of Charles I, Berkeley declared the succession of Charles II to the throne and Virginia's support for him. But Berkeley also asserted Virginia's ongoing autonomy in trade (open trade with the Dutch was providing some economic stability for the colony) and self-governance of the colony on local matters. Nevertheless, Charles II was soon ousted as king, Parliament turned England into a republic, and Berkeley was removed from office in 1652 by commissioners sent by Parliament. Yet despite Parliament's institution of the Navigation Acts, which sought to reestablish England's monopoly

FIGURE 2.1
The Third Statehouse, Jamestown, ca. 1675 (from Charles E. Hatch, *America's Oldest Legislative Assembly & Its Jamestown Statehouses* [1956])

over all trade to and from Virginia, little actually changed in the colony. Indeed, Parliament gave Virginians the right to choose their own governor, and in 1660, they restored Berkeley to the governorship after having been ruled by two others in the 1650s.

While Berkeley was generally respected in the colony, the 1660s and 1670s posed special challenges to his administration. In the first place, Virginia's ongoing reliance on tobacco was increasingly problematic. Dutch buyers in the 1640s and '50s helped keep the market afloat, but after 1660, Parliament renewed its earlier Navigation Acts and made effective efforts to enforce them. Berkeley took it upon himself to break Virginia's dependence on tobacco and made a concerted effort at reducing the colony's tobacco production while diversifying its agriculture. Even through Berkeley had the Crown and Parliament's tacit approval and the support of the House of Burgesses, the governor found tobacco's sway over the colony to be too powerful to overcome.

Meanwhile, England and the Netherlands went to war twice in the mid-1660s and mid-1670s. Berkeley acquitted himself well in his defense of Virginia, but the Crown's defensive strategy did little to actually aid the colony. Berkeley and the assembly were forced to raise taxes to mount a defense, ultimately constructing useless forts on poorly chosen ground (such as building a fort on the swampy Point Comfort, which overlooked the entrance to the James River).

Throughout this period, Berkeley maintained the support of his government. The council, of course, consisted of those appointed by Berkeley himself. In order to keep the support of the burgesses, Berkeley chose not to call new elections after 1662. Despite significant population growth, and a shift in the population such that some 20 percent of the residents now hailed from the Northern Neck, the burgesses formed a "Long Assembly" from 1662–76. Newcomers had little voice as a result, but Berkeley could work with a group of men who knew and trusted him.

Berkeley's Virginia pitted the well-to-do against one another in profound ways. While one might assume that the basic conflict in Virginia was between the elite and those of lower social status, the situation was more complicated. Those who held political power did not necessarily come from higher social status in England, though they had become close with Governor Berkeley. Consider the case of William Drummond, who came to the colony as an indentured servant but then rose to prominence as landowner, merchant, and eventually governor of the newly emerging Carolina colony. But after a falling out with Berkeley, he lost much of his political power and social standing. In contrast, Giles Bland came to the colony with English social standing and with claims to a relative's Virginia lands, but he quickly irritated and alienated members of Berkeley's inner circle and Berkeley himself. The council of state soon stripped him of his office of customs collector. Despite their different social origins, Bland and Drummond shared an exclusion from Virginia's power structures.

"He That Lives in the Nature of a Servant": Virginia's Sociopolitical Hierarchy, Social Unrest, and Rising Tensions
The Social Hierarchy of Colonial Virginia

Over the decades, Virginia had developed into a society that mirrored England's social hierarchy while also exhibiting its own distinctive character. As detailed in figure 2.2, all Virginians fell into a pecking order where economic and political power was concentrated among those who resided in the apex of the pyramid. Generally speaking, the further from the top one sat in the hierarchy, the more disempowered such an individual was.

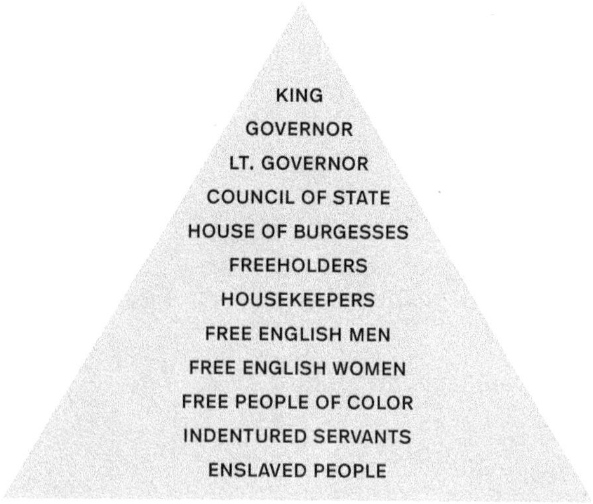

While this chart conveys a basic sense of Virginia's social hierarchy, the situation was more complicated than this, particularly at the top rungs and in the lower rungs. The upper echelon was composed of those with social *and* political prestige. The combination of wealth and political power tended to push individuals higher up the ladder, but the line between freeholders and members of the House of Burgesses was somewhat muddled. There certainly existed individuals of significant financial means who came from high social standing in England but did not hold political office, while at the same time several burgesses and even some councillors had less wealth than those who were not in office. This was one of the reasons for the tensions in Virginia, since Berkeley's supporters tended to hold political office while others of higher English social standing were politically excluded.

The lower rungs were even more muddled, since free people of color undoubtedly were economically better off than indentured servants of any race (and were legally free), but the racial attitudes of the English tended to demean their position while the law prevented them from rising above freeman status. Indeed, white indentured servants had been known to not only gain their freedom but rise through the ranks of Virginia's economic and political elite. No Afro-Virginian, it seemed, could ever hope to do that. The line between enslaved people and indentured servants was also confused. Only Afro-Virginians were enslaved, but some had been able to move up to freeman status. Anglo-Virginians who were indentured servants could expect to eventually gain their freedom and never had to worry about becoming enslaved. Yet the few Afro-Virginians who were indentured and held hope for freedom also knew that bad luck might lead to their relegation as slaves. As the decades wore on, the lines between these categories became more rigidly race-based, and Afro-Virginians found fewer and fewer opportunities for advancement.

Patronage significantly contributed to Virginia's social class system. The governor received his office from the king (an expression of the king's patronage) and in turn granted offices to those he favored. These positions consisted first and foremost of seats on the council, which offered its members many economic opportunities as well as service on the final court of appeal in the colony. The governor also appointed local magistrates—usually judges in the county courts—who wielded significant power in their neighborhoods. While the salaries associated with the appointments were important, more significant

KING
GOVERNOR
LT. GOVERNOR
COUNCIL OF STATE
HOUSE OF BURGESSES
FREEHOLDERS
HOUSEKEEPERS
FREE ENGLISH MEN
FREE ENGLISH WOMEN
FREE PEOPLE OF COLOR
INDENTURED SERVANTS
ENSLAVED PEOPLE

FIGURE 2.2 Virginia's social and political hierarchy

were the opportunities the positions presented the holders. Referring to his position as a collector of navigation duties, Nicholas Spencer observed that "the proffit of salary is not soe much as the many advantages it gives mee otherwayes."[7]

Patronage also contributed to the social hierarchy through the granting of labor and the best parcels of land. Those with the most political power—the governor and members of the council—usually owned the most servants and slaves and had the largest tracts of land, typically located closest to the navigable portions of Virginia's rivers (giving them direct access to shipping tobacco and receiving goods).

But it is important to observe that Virginia's elite, especially those who held political power and benefitted from Berkeley's patronage, did not always parallel the elite of England. Many of Berkeley's ardent supporters were self-made men who had come to the colony as indentured servants and who made their way up Virginia's social ranks through the strength of their own efforts, not just through the governor's patronage. Consequently, when men of economic means and English social status arrived in the colony, they often discovered that their position back home did not open the same doors of opportunity for them in Virginia. Indeed, they frequently found themselves in competition with individuals who they considered their social inferiors.

Frustrations of the Freedmen

The increasing concentration of wealth and power in the hands of the elite meant increased pressures on those below. The system worked well while accessible arable land was available and opportunities for advancement seemed within the grasp of the common (white) Virginian, but as the seventeenth century wore on, such land and opportunity became more and more limited.

Improved survivability and demographic shifts contributed to these limitations. Virginia's mortality rate was particularly high in its early years. Between 1625 and 1640, some 15,000 people migrated to the colony, but just over half of these survived. Disease was primarily responsible for the high death rate, although many also died in the Indian wars and some from the conditions of their labor. However, after 1640, death rates declined and the population rose, reaching over 25,000 by 1662.

In the 1660s and 1670s, growing numbers of freedmen sought land but met several obstacles. Available plots could only be found inland, away from the rivers, above the rivers' fall lines (the point at which ocean-going vessels could not pass), or exposed to potentially hostile Native Americans. Land that met the necessary requirements was expensive and out of reach for the newly freed laborers.

Absent the opportunity for land, these freedmen sought other opportunities. Some chose to work as free laborers. They worked for wages, hoping to earn enough to purchase farms of their own. Others became vagabonds and drifters. By 1676, one-fourth of the colony's freedmen were landless. This class mostly comprised single, young men, and they were increasingly impatient, armed, and rebellious.

Problems of the Planters

Even planters on established lands faced challenges to their livelihood and their hopes for the future. Chiefly, tobacco prices were again depressed after 1670 due to overproduction and limits on exports resulting from the recent Navigation Acts. Prices made an even sharper decline in 1675. Added to reduced profits was the addition of oppressive levies, many established in response to the defensive needs of the colony during the Anglo-Dutch Wars of 1652–54, 1665–67, and 1672–74. These taxes, of course, affected the freedmen, too, and led to a shared discontent of the establishment. Both freedmen and planters who did not have a place on the council of state or even a seat in the House of Burgesses became increasingly bitter for having to pay higher taxes while Berkeley and his cronies lived extravagant lifestyles.

In fact, Berkeley's system of patronage provided opportunity for a select few while disaffecting many others. While most colonists paid taxes, others were given significant tax exemptions. The political offices granted by Berkeley could be quite profitable, including access to quality lands, tax breaks, and wages for public service. By 1676, many colonists were fed up with Berkeley. It was bad enough that he dominated politics at the center of the colony, but through the influence of his patronage, he was able to control county politics in the appointment of sheriffs and justices. Anyone who was not in Berkeley's camp—rich or middling—had little say in either local or colonial affairs, but small farmers especially resented the power of a few wealthy families, many of whom were related to each other not just through patronage but also through marriage.

Even newcomers with connections to Governor Berkeley, such as Nathaniel Bacon, found only limited opportunities. Related to Berkeley through the governor's wife, Lady Frances, Bacon came to the colony with money in his pocket and was received by the governor with open arms. In fact, Berkeley soon appointed Bacon to the council of state. Yet even with such resources at his disposal, Bacon could only establish himself far up the James River, distant from the ocean-going trade vessels and the centers of power at Jamestown. Meanwhile, his backcountry plantation and farms put his property at greater risk of attacks from Native Americans. And while such a location had potential for benefiting from the Indian trade, Berkeley and his supporters sought to control such trade for their own benefit.

Social Unrest: Servants and Slaves

During the first thirty years of Virginia's history, indentured servitude had been a successful labor strategy, at least from the standpoint of those who held property and sought affordable and reliable labor. Servants were cheaper than slaves, and few lived to see their freedom when they would become competitors for land and opportunity. And even though some slave ships made their way to Virginia's shores in those decades, England was not greatly involved in the transatlantic slave trade, rendering African slaves scarce and expensive.

But demands for labor in a society driven essentially by greed and a quest for social, economic, and political advancement meant great hardship for servants. Indentured servants often served longer terms of service than required by their contracts and were often abused by their masters. Masters, aided and abetted by local courts, had exceptional latitude in the treatment of their servants. The courts often added time to their contracts as punishment for various infractions. In these ways, their servitude was much more severe in Virginia than in England. Some tried legal means to ameliorate their plight by suing masters for clothes, proper medical care, fulfillment of contract, honoring agreements to teach a trade, and redress for physical abuse. Some were successful, and others were reprimanded with extended terms.

This provoked many to seek extralegal means of expressing their political and social discontent. For example, in York County in 1661, a group of indentured servants plotted to revolt against authorities. Led by Isaac Friend and William Clutton, whose indentures belonged to Maj. James Goodwin, this group was angered by the lack of meat in their diet. But their conspiracy was apparently revealed before they could act. The county court warned Friend about his behavior and encouraged his overseer to watch him more carefully. Clutton was arrested for delivering "seditious words & speeches," although the result of the county's legal action is not known.

Two years later, nine indentured servants in Gloucester County met in the woods and planned to secure arms, ammunition, and a drum from a councillor's plantation and, with perhaps as many as thirty recruits, marched on the governor's mansion at Green Spring to demand release from their indentures. If the governor refused, they were prepared to kill him. However, a servant named Birkenhead betrayed them; they were ambushed at their meeting place, and the captured servants were tried by the General Court and hanged for treason. After rewarding Birkenhead with his freedom and 5,000 pounds of tobacco, the Grand Assembly declared that the day of their planned insurrection would be celebrated annually, on September 13. (See the court records relating to the Gloucester Conspiracy among the core texts.)

Enslaved Africans had even greater reason to rebel since their status was degrading over time. Anglo-

Virginian fear of such rebellion only worsened their plight. Most significantly, in 1672, the Grand Assembly approved an act permitting the killing of enslaved Africans, as well as Indian and mulatto servants, for running away or for criminal activity—an act that served to divide servants along a color line.

"For the Lord's Sake Shoot No More, These Are Our Friends the Susquehannocks": Native American–Anglo-Virginian Conflict, 1675–1676

Added to the political, social, and economic frustrations of Anglo- and Afro-Virginians were renewed conflicts with Virginia's Native American neighbors. The constant pressure of settler colonialism on Native people led to physical displacements, aggravated conflict between Native groups, competition for natural resources and trade with Europeans, and increased friction between the tribes and their English neighbors. Desperation on the part of Native Americans and racial animosity on the part of Europeans led to thievery, raids, attacks, and enmity on both sides.

A vicious cycle of violence, tension, and unease emerged, especially on the frontier—the zone of close contact between English settlements and the Native communities not subdued in earlier wars. Many English colonists on the frontier wished for aggressive military action against these Indians. But conflict on the frontier did not threaten the heart of the colony, so government responses were tempered and moderate. To the majority of colonists, the colonial government in Jamestown seemed inept and negligent in their handling of Indian affairs. It was certainly not in the interest of Berkeley and his clique to pursue offensive war against the Indians. Not only would it be costly, but such a war would adversely affect trade relations, hampering the elite's income and profits derived from their monopoly on the Indian trade.

The Doegs and the Susquehannocks

In 1675, however, conflict on the Virginia and Maryland frontiers involving two Native American groups escalated to the point of war. The Algonquian-speaking Doegs (pronounced *doge* to rhyme with *rogue*) were natives of the Chesapeake region, particularly the Northern Neck, between the Rappahannock and Potomac Rivers, and the upper reaches of those rivers. As English colonists moved into the area, they competed with the Doeg and other tribes for the land. In fact, the Doeg and others resisted, resulting in the Anglo-Virginians declaring war on them in 1666. Consequently, the Doeg were displaced to the Maryland side of the Potomac, although they continued to trade and interact with the English colonists.

Sometime in 1675, Thomas Mathew, a settler on the Northern Neck, failed to pay some Doegs for goods he purchased from them. In July, several Doegs crossed the Potomac to his plantation, captured multiple hogs, and began transporting them back across the river in their dugouts. The English gave pursuit in a sailboat. After catching up to them, both sides launched volleys of their respective weapons—English muskets and Native bows—but the Indians were outmatched. Some toppled into the water after being shot while others were beaten once the boats made contact. The English retrieved their livestock while the Indians straggled back to their side of the river.

But the Doegs apparently sought revenge several weeks later. On a Sunday morning, some settlers passed the cabin of Robert Hen, one of Mathew's employees, and found Hen badly wounded and a slain Indian nearby, both victims of hatchet blows. With his final breaths, Hen identified the attackers: Doegs.

The militia was called up, but the results of the battle had unintended consequences. Col. George Mason and Capt. George Brent led the troops in pursuit of the retreating war party and tracked them upriver some twenty miles and then across into Maryland. There, Brent's force surrounded one cabin and called for a parley. When the Doeg leader emerged, the captain seized him by "his twisted lock (which was all the hair he wore)" and demanded he turn over "the Murderer of Robert Hen," but the man escaped his grip and tried to flee.[8] Brent shot him down, the Doegs within the cabin opened fire, and the militia responded. Surrounded and outgunned, the Doegs fled the cabin amid the militia's gunfire, leaving some ten dead or mortally wounded.

Meanwhile, Mason's group surrounded another nearby cabin. Upon being wakened by the sound of gunfire from the first group, the inhabitants of this cabin stumbled out of doors, only to have fourteen of them mowed down by Mason's men. One managed to reach Mason, grasping for his arm, and exclaimed "Susquehanougs Netoughs" ("Susquehannock friends")![9]

Indeed, these were not Doegs, but Susquehannocks, and the Susquehannocks were friends of both Maryland and Virginia. An Iroquoian-speaking people, this nation had once comprised the most populous Indigenous group inhabiting the Susquehanna Valley at the time of contact with Europeans. Through the mid-seventeenth century, they had held a position of relative strength, maintaining an active role in the fur trade with Europeans. In 1652, they established an alliance with Maryland. Such an arrangement provided them with trade privileges and guns that would help them defend against Native incursions from the north and east; for the Marylanders, the Susquehannocks provided a defensive buffer on their northern boundaries. Indeed, in the 1650s and 1660s, the Susquehannocks were in the ascendancy despite endemic warfare with the Iroquois Confederacy. But in the early 1670s, many of their communities were struck by devastating epidemics of unintentionally introduced European disease.

Realizing the horrible error, Mason quickly "ran amongst the Men, Crying out 'For the Lord's sake Shoot no more, these are our friends the Susquehanoughs,'" but the damage was done (see Thomas Mathew, "The Beginning, Progress, and Conclusion of Bacon's Rebellion, 1675–1676," core text). Although the Susquehannocks had a beneficial relationship with Maryland and Virginia and relied on their largesse in order to establish a secure territory for themselves, the grievous loss of their people's lives at the cabin had to be accounted for. Unlike European standards of justice, in which offenders of the crime of murder should be tried and pay the penalty for their crime, the Susquehannocks and many Native people of the region sought to "requicken" the dead—to replace them with individuals captured from other communities or to have their losses compensated by similar losses among the enemy. So they attacked some outlying settlements, killing two Virginians and several Marylanders. They then established themselves in a fortified camp near the mouth of Piscataway Creek on the Maryland side of the Potomac River.

Escalation

Virginia and Maryland could not accept the Susquehannocks' method for resolving the murder of their people at the cabin, so they escalated the conflict. Moreover, word of the so-called King Philip's War in New England began to reach the Chesapeake. In June 1675, some Pokanoket Indians attacked the Plymouth settlement of Swansea after the murder of a Massachusett Indian informer and an ensuing trial and execution of several Wampanoags for the deed. Over the coming months, English and Indian forces from various New England tribes attacked and counterattacked, destroying Native villages and English settlements respectively. The English blamed Metacom, leader of the Wampanoags, who was known by the English as King Philip. They asserted that he was coordinating a rebellion among the New England tribes; in reality, the various Algonquian-speaking groups had long-standing grievances that they were addressing through military resistance. Hearing news of this war, Governor Berkeley feared that local Indian uprisings were part of a broader, coordinated Native American effort throughout the English colonies. He and Maryland governor, Lord Baltimore, called up militia troops led by John Washington and Isaac Allerton Jr. for Virginia and Maj. Thomas Truman for Maryland.

They found 100 warriors encamped with some 400 women, children, and others, but neither a decisive diplomatic nor military decision resulted from their meeting. Initially engaging in negotiations with the

Susquehannocks, the English became impatient with the process, and John Washington suggested "let us knock [the emissaries] on the head [and] we shall get the forte to day."[10] They did, in fact, do this to the Susquehannock diplomats and then set a siege about the village. In the late summer and early fall, English attempts to breach the fortified village failed, while warriors often snuck out at night, killed English troops, and stole tools and weapons. Finally, in November, all the Susquehannocks slipped out of the fort at night and fled the region, poised for revenge.

The Susquehannocks fled south to Virginia's backcountry and beyond and distributed their people among several camps. By December, one group settled above the James River falls, a second group settled southwest of the Virginia colony, two other groups settled along the Roanoke River, while yet another group settled north of Maryland. In January (1676 by modern calendars), Susquehannock men entered northern Virginia and made a series of attacks, killing between thirty-six and sixty colonists on small isolated farms along the Rappahannock River, and then returned to their winter camps satisfied. A group of raiders on their way back from the Rappahannock attacks descended on Bacon's Quarter, Nathaniel Bacon's trading outpost and tobacco field close to the James River falls. In the struggle, Bacon's overseer was murdered and the plantation razed. The raiders killed and tortured other residents in the area before retreating.

At this point, the Susquehannocks again sought peace, but a rapprochement with Virginia would not be forthcoming. Although the Susquehannocks declared themselves satisfied and called for an end to hostilities, Berkeley could not now renew peace with the Susquehannocks given the death and destruction they had recently wrought. Although the Virginians and Marylanders may have aggrieved the Susquehannocks initially, English officials would not condone the Native peoples' unilateral execution of justice. After an emergency meeting in Jamestown, Governor Berkeley and the council of state charged Lieutenant Governor Sir Henry Chicheley with tracking down the Susquehannock raiders. But after

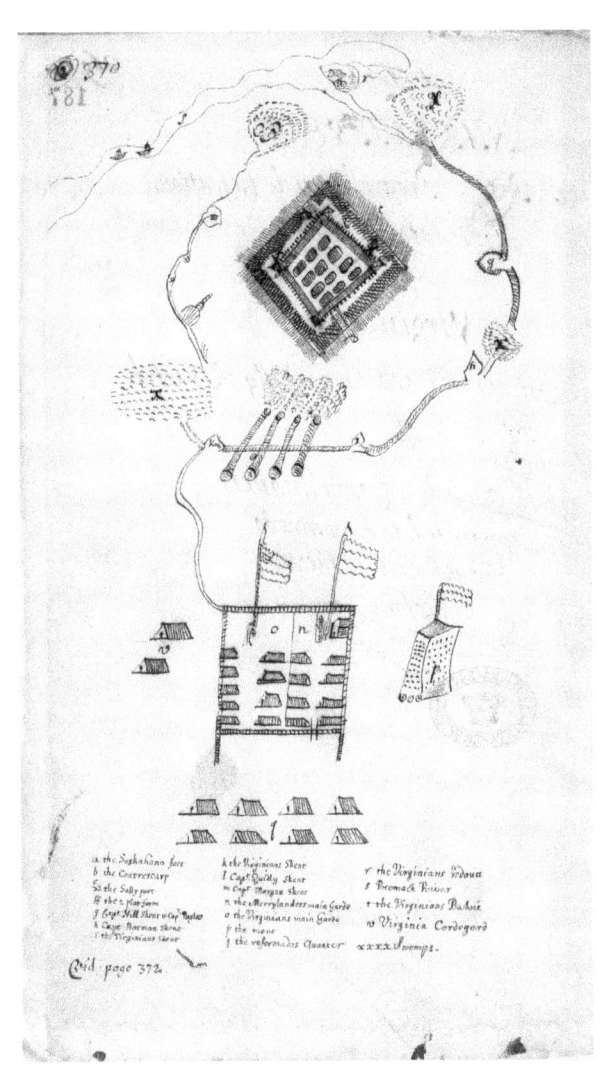

FIGURE 2.3 Sketch of Susquehannock fort and siege by an English observer (British National Archives)

Chicheley mustered 300 men and prepared to avenge the recent murders of their fellow Virginians, the governor inexplicably rescinded his orders. This left many Virginians, particularly those living in the backcountry, frustrated and unhappy, including Nathaniel Bacon.

Berkeley then called the House of Burgesses to meet with the council of state in a Grand Assembly meant to address Indian affairs. Fearful of a colony-destroying war such as New England was then experiencing, Berkeley also could not abide the impudence of the Susquehannocks and the Doegs. But he

HISTORICAL BACKGROUND 31

and his allies did not want to see the lucrative Indian trade (deer skins, food stuffs, slaves) disrupted. Worsening the situation was the ongoing social unrest in the colony. With thoughts of the English Civil War in the back of Berkeley's mind, he was quite concerned about the possible breakdown of the social and political order. Working through the assembly, he hoped a path forward could be found to end the Indian hostilities while maintaining the political and social status quo.

3
The Game

MAJOR ISSUES FOR DEBATE

Governor Berkeley has called a special session of the Grand Assembly for March 6, 1676, after a fifteen-year hiatus, hence the nickname "The Long Assembly" (since the last elections). The governor offers a proposal in response to recent rumors, raids, and complaints concerning "The Indian Problem." The initial debate of the game centers upon the best policy for securing the safety and defense of the Virginia backcountry.

Defensive Approach

Supporters of this approach—Berkeley and others—are unalterably AGAINST any action that might bring about further conflict with Native Americans. Regulated trade and good relations with peaceful Native groups is essential. Raids on the frontier are the responsibility of a handful of Natives who should be taken care of by means other than outright war and excessive force. Therefore, a defensive approach to the Native American crisis is warranted—secure the borders and prevent any invasions through the building and manning of a series of forts and through the use of regular armed patrols. An overly aggressive approach to the recent conflict will only set off widespread anti-European Indian resistance akin to King Philip's War in New England. Offensive attacks and indiscriminate slaughter of tribes will exacerbate tensions and cause violence between the colonists and Native neighbors.

Offensive Approach

Supporters of this approach—Bacon and others—are not satisfied by the government's actions and *inactions* that have given Native Americans an open door to attack the backcountry plantations. Because of increasing violence and rumors of more raids, murder, and torture from Native Americans along the edge of the settlements, immediate action is necessary and long overdue. Therefore, an offensive approach for the safety and defense of the frontier is warranted, and only total annihilation of the Native American threat will prevent further bloodshed and invasion. Furthermore, supporters of this approach are AGAINST regulated trade and alliances with Native Americans. The frontier should be made secure against Indians, the land opened up for settlement, and trade allowed between anyone.

OTHER ISSUES FOR DEBATE

Yet the preoccupation with Indian affairs has blinded many in the government to the simmering tensions throughout the colony. But not so for the rest of the colony's residents. The calling of the Grand Assembly after so many years has created an opportunity for its members and others in the colony to address their most pressing concerns. Consequently, the following issues will likely emerge as the game develops.

- Control of the corn trade. In order to make a living, many planters and farmers depend on corn production along with, or in place of, tobacco production. But in times of war, when food may be scarce, government efforts to secure the supply of corn (and regulate its price) may be necessary (but may also threaten the livelihood of some farmers).
- Free laborers. Can landless men really be productive and orderly members of colonial society? How to appease and keep them from upsetting the established order?
- Indentured servants. Land can no longer be guaranteed upon freedom. What is the place for landless white men in colonial Virginia? What actions can the Grand Assembly take to improve servants' lot and chances for success after service?
- Enslaved people. The assembly has already ruled on slavery, making it a lifetime term, regardless of conversion to Christianity or birth to a free father. Should this law be rescinded, maintained, or expanded? Should some or all slaves be freed, and if so, with what conditions?
- Free people of color. Should they be allowed to become freeholders with the right to vote despite not being ethnically or racially English? Should legal freedom mean political equality? Where do people of color belong in the hierarchy of English colonial society?

- Women. With its high mortality rate, Virginia has more than its share of orphans and widows. Some widows who control property wonder whether women should be freeholders as well. And Afro-Virginian women ask, should there be legal distinctions between themselves and Anglo-Virginian women?

RULES AND PROCEDURES

Objectives and Victory Conditions

There are two tracks to victory in this game. First, all characters have their own set of objectives outlined in their respective role sheets. Unless stated otherwise, you can achieve victory by meeting a majority of these conditions, regardless of the outcome of your faction's victory conditions.

Players can also win the game collectively through a faction victory. By the end of the game, all players will be aligned either with Governor Berkeley or Nathaniel Bacon. While players cannot ignore individual victory conditions, it is generally true that members of the faction who control Virginia at the end of the game win. (Note: In the standard game, control of Jamestown stands in for control of the whole colony.)

The Grand Assembly

Most of the game action takes place in the Virginia statehouse, located in Jamestown, where the Grand Assembly meets. The assembly is made up of the House of Burgesses, the council of state (including the lieutenant governor), and Governor Berkeley.

Layout of the classroom. To approximate the arrangement of the statehouse, the classroom should be set up so that the council of state, the Speaker of the assembly (who was himself a burgess), and the governor sit in the front area facing the rest of the room. Facing them in the front row of the room will be seated members of the House of Burgesses. In a separate area, clearly distinguished from the members of the Grand Assembly, should be the gallery where nonvoting Virginians and invited guests are permitted to sit (or stand or walk as they choose).

Furthermore, characters who are people of color should sit farthest back and distinct from Anglo-Virginians. White women characters should sit adjacent to the men, rather than comingle with members of the opposite sex to whom they are not wed.

The council of state. In colonial Virginia, the council was appointed by the governor and had the power along with him of approving or vetoing laws

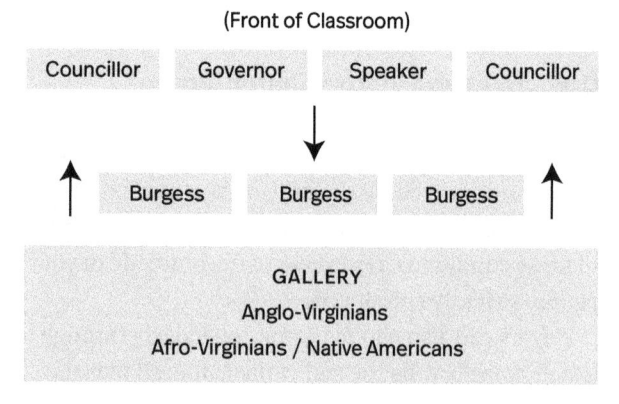

```
                (Front of Classroom)
    ┌──────────┬──────────┬──────────┬──────────┐
    │Councillor│ Governor │ Speaker  │Councillor│
    └──────────┴──────────┴──────────┴──────────┘
                         │
                         ▼
         ┌─────────┬─────────┬─────────┐
    ↑    │ Burgess │ Burgess │ Burgess │    ↑
         └─────────┴─────────┴─────────┘
         ┌─────────────────────────────┐
         │          GALLERY            │
         │      Anglo-Virginians       │
         │ Afro-Virginians / Native Americans │
         └─────────────────────────────┘
```

FIGURE 3.1 Recommended classroom layout (arrows indicate direction players face during assembly meetings)

passed by the burgesses. In this game, however, the legislative process has been simplified by having members of the council and the burgesses vote together. In order to simulate the power council members wield relative to the burgesses, each time a councillor or the Speaker votes, five votes are cast. Henry Chicheley, the lieutenant governor, in recognition of his additional authority and political status, casts eight votes. Since these votes represent the political power of the character and not a group of people they represent, these votes cannot be split. In other words, a councillor may not cast two votes in favor of a measure while also casting three votes against.

The House of Burgesses. In contrast to the council members, the burgesses are elected by the white property-holding males—freeholders. Burgesses each cast a single vote.

The gallery. Every character in the game is welcome to attend the deliberations of the Grand Assembly as members of the gallery. These freeholders who do not hold office, free laborers, free people of color, free women, indentured servants, enslaved people, and Native Americans are not allowed to vote, however.

The Speaker. Every Grand Assembly session is chaired by the Speaker: the moderator or presiding officer of the assembly. Normally, the assembly itself elects the Speaker, but since it has not met since 1660, and the former Speaker has recently died, the governor has appointed Col. Augustine Warner Jr. to the position. His duties include the following:

- Make sure that all the topics listed on the schedule for each session are addressed and receive equal treatment in terms of debate.
- Recognize and introduce speakers, including members from the gallery, at the podium.
- Manage debates.
- Ensure that proposals are written and distributed before being voted upon.
- Manage amendments to proposals.
- Count votes and announce results.

As a burgess, the Speaker also votes, but his political influence as moderator of the Grand Assembly is reflected in his ability to cast five votes.

The Speaker can be removed from his position as the result of a majority vote of "no confidence" at any time. Should a burgess wish to do so, he must stand, call for a vote of no confidence, and briefly explain his rationale. If it is seconded by another member of the Grand Assembly, the GM will moderate the no-confidence proceedings. If it is not seconded, business continues as usual.

During the no-confidence vote, the Speaker may not cast a vote in that decision. If it passes, the Grand Assembly must elect a new Speaker through nominations and a majority vote. *The new Speaker must be nominated from among the burgesses.* The former Speaker may vote in this election, but now only has a single vote. The councillors also may cast votes in favor of their preferred Speaker. Once elected, the new Speaker has the power to cast five votes just as the former Speaker had.

If the Speaker is absent, the governor must appoint a temporary replacement from among the burgesses. While Speaker, this temporary replacement also casts five votes.

The governor. As a representative of the Crown, the governor is the supreme political authority in the colony. Even so, he does not vote with members of the Grand Assembly. His power is evident, however, in his ability to break ties, approve measures that receive only a plurality of votes, and veto legislation in rare circumstances (only he knows when he might use this power). See details under "Voting in the assembly."

Additional Rules of the Grand Assembly

Virginia was a sharply hierarchical society, just like England at the time. The social structures reflected this hierarchy as was particularly evident in the practices of the Grand Assembly. At the beginning of each session of the colonial legislature, members enter following a distinct ritual outlined below. In short, those with the greatest privilege and of the highest social standing enter the room last but sit closest to (or at) the front. Although it may seem backward by modern-day standards, such practice was common in the era and ensures that the lower classes wait upon the upper classes and not the reverse.

The procedure is this: before the assembly sessions begin, the governor, councillors, and burgesses should go outside the classroom or separate themselves in some way from other members of the class. The sergeant at arms (Drummond) will command all in attendance to stand and be quiet and does the following:

1. In a loud voice, he will announce, "The members of the House of Burgesses!," after which the burgesses will enter and stand at their designated place.
2. Then he will announce, "Their honors, the councillors of state," who will enter and stand at their places.
3. Finally, he will call out, "His excellency, the governor," who will enter and take his place at the front.

Each should enter at a leisurely pace and with a strong sense of dignity and entitlement. Once the governor sits, the councillors follow. Then the burgesses may sit, and finally the members of the gallery. In order to reinforce the social ranking of the characters, the GM may ask players to don certain clothing elements or distribute such garb to them.

Respect the podium. Once standing at the podium, any character has the right to speak. In Reacting games, the common practice is for players to stand in line behind the speaker at the podium and wait for their turn to speak, time permitting. But GMs and speakers may adopt other means to organize those wishing to address the room. When speaking for the first time in the assembly, speakers should at least identify their names and titles.

However, in seventeenth-century Virginia, the presence of women or people of color on the floor of the assembly would be unexpected, to say the least, so such individuals may not speak without being sponsored at the podium by a member of the Grand Assembly or by express permission of the Speaker. There are some legislators who are willing to champion the cause of these disempowered individuals or who will at least support their right to speak. In order to be heard, then, some characters must enlist the aid of others. When a nonwhite male or any female wishes to speak, their advocate in the assembly will come to the podium and announce that they are sponsoring that individual and then yield the floor to them (invite them to take their place at the podium and speak).

Speakers may not filibuster—that is, they must yield the podium after a reasonable time has passed (to be determined by the Speaker and GM) rather than speak so long as to prevent others from speaking or thwart any legislative business from being completed.

Once completing a speech, the character at the podium should remain there and address any questions as moderated by the Speaker. Anyone in the gallery or in the assembly may question individuals at the podium (although the Speaker of the assembly may grant this right to assemblymen before others).

Other ways to be heard. While those at the podium must be allowed to speak, it is expected that members of the assembly and gallery will audibly express their support or disapproval of what is said by hissing, booing, cheering, shouting "hear, hear," rapping on tabletops, and so forth. While this is strongly encouraged, players should be aware that the Speaker may enlist the sergeant at arms to quell any unruliness that becomes disruptive of constructive debate. None should be surprised if the Speaker has a higher standard of what is considered unruly when applied to Afro-Virginians; this is in keeping with the racial attitudes of your typical Anglo-Virginian.

Drafting proposals. In order to be considered by the assembly, proposals must be written out in the exact language in which they are to be adopted (see below for examples). Players are encouraged to draft proposals *before* legislative sessions and to organize speeches in support of them. Ideally, sufficient copies should be provided to voting members of the assembly. To avoid confusion, proposals must be concise and written in contemporary language; they should focus on the essentials and omit the technical details.

There are two types of legislation in proposals: acts and resolutions. **Acts** are laws that require certain actions. **Resolutions** are nonbinding declarations that do not require action.

- Example of a proposed act: In order to secure the safety and property of the residents of Virginia, forts for defense shall be built at the falls of each navigable river in the colony.
- Example of a proposed resolution: In recognition of the honorable service Governor Berkeley has provided the colony, the assembly hereby declares their loyalty to him.

During sessions, amendments may be added to the proposals. If the proposed amendment is acceptable to the author of the proposal (a so-called friendly amendment), the legislation is to be considered as amended. If it is not approved by the proposal's author, then the amendment must be voted on before considering the legislation and will pass with a simple majority.

Voting in the assembly. Only elected members of the House of Burgesses and appointed members of the council of state are allowed to vote; these are all noted above. Voting is carried out by raised hands or vote cards and counted by the Speaker or an appointed assistant. No proxy or absentee votes are allowed. Thus, in any given session, the possible number of votes equals the sum of the votes available to players who are present at a game session.

Eligible voters may vote "yes," "no," or "abstain." The governor does not cast a vote, but may break a tie. *Acts and resolutions are passed by simple majority of total possible votes in a given session, including abstentions* (anyone with voting power who does not vote effectively abstains). By definition, a majority is 50 percent of the possible votes plus one. Thus if there are seventeen votes possible in a session, at least nine votes must be cast in favor of a proposal for it to pass.

TIP Always count the number of possible votes after everyone has arrived for a session in case someone is absent and changes the calculation for a majority vote.

Having more *ayes* than *nays* but 50 percent or fewer of possible votes is called a *plurality*. In the example above, a plurality would result from eight ayes, five nays, and four abstentions. A particular measure in this case will not pass. However, the governor's tiebreaking power also applies to these circumstances—he can always declare a measure passed even if it has received a plurality of votes.

Table 3.1 lists eligible voters in the assembly at the start of the game according to class size. Note that the composition of the Grand Assembly can change during the game.

The governor's veto. Reminder: The governor possesses the power to veto legislation that has been passed by a majority vote, but this power is limited and only the governor (and GM) knows when he may wield it. When issuing a veto, the governor must deliver an explanation; the Grand Assembly cannot override the veto.

TABLE 3.1 Characters with voting power

Size of class	Character	Number of votes in assembly
12–18	Sir William Berkeley (governor)	tie breaker
	Col. Philip Ludwell (councillor)	5
	Nathaniel Bacon (councillor)	5
	Col. John Washington (burgess)	1
	Col. John West II (burgess)	1
	Col. Augustine Warner Jr. (burgess)	5 (as Speaker)
19–21	Sir Henry Chicheley (lieutenant governor)	7
22–23	Col. Thomas Ballard (councillor)	5
24	Maj. Robert Beverley (burgess)	1
25–26	Col. Nicholas Spencer Jr. (councillor)	5
27	Richard Lawrence (burgess)	1
28	Col. Edward Hill (burgess)	1
29–30	Maj. Isaac Allerton Jr. (burgess)	1

How to Join a Faction

At the beginning of the game, at least half of the characters are independents; the rest are permanent members of either the Bacon or Berkeley faction. After the second legislative session, all characters must officially join a faction. This moment in the game is called the Loyalty Phase. To officially join a faction, you must sign a loyalty oath to Berkeley or Bacon.

You should consider your reasons for joining a particular faction. You may be convinced of the justice of the positions they represent, or you may simply support the side that you think is likely to win. You may also choose sides based on personal deals that help you meet your other victory conditions.

Note that you do not need to wait until the Loyalty Phase to commit to a faction; you may join at any time up to that point. Furthermore, all indeterminates may change sides throughout the game up until the Loyalty Phase, at which point your name is inscribed upon the loyalty oath. To do so, you must inform the leader of the faction you are joining and ALSO inform the GM. You are not required to inform the leader of a faction if you are leaving. However, *if you have accepted a personal deal in exchange for your loyalty earlier in the game, you lose that benefit when you change sides*. Additionally, when characters change factions, there may be negative consequences for either the character or the faction. Thus, joining and switching sides should not be undertaken lightly.

If the extended version of the game is played, characters may switch sides during the campaigns following Jamestown, but once the war is over, they must remain with whichever faction they fought alongside in the final campaign.

Militias

During colonial America, most able-bodied men were members of the militia. Individual towns and counties formed local independent militias for their own defense. These militias were led by individual officers—usually colonels—and supported and assisted by subordinate officers (majors and captains), who could also assume command in the case of absence or death of colonels.

In times of emergency, the governor would mobilize militias, but in a time of crisis such as in 1676, the potential for the militias to self-mobilize or to be mobilized by someone other than the governor (e.g., Bacon) was great. Should political solutions not be found for the problems facing Virginia, the militias could become very important. Thus, faction leaders should pay attention to how the militia officers are politically aligned and should work to recruit them to their side.

TIP Faction leaders should pay attention to how the militia officers are politically aligned and should work to recruit them to their side.

While militia officers have significant military strength (see below), all free white men in the game possess military ability and therefore carry military strength points in time of war. The military strength points consist of their individual military ability as well as their representative military power—that is, the relative strength of those they represent. For example, an enlisted man has 5 strength points, 1 for himself and 4 for people of similar status he represents. Similarly, for each slave and indentured servant in the game, should they become enlisted in the military for one side or another, they represent several other persons of the same status who are not actually present in the game.

Military strength generally follows this scheme:

- Colonels: 20 points
- Majors: 15 points
- Captains: 10 points
- All other English freemen: 5 points

As lieutenant general of the colonial militia, Henry Chicheley commands 30 strength points.

As leaders of their respective factions, Governor Berkeley and Nathaniel Bacon each contribute military power in the event of a military conflict, but this power is known only to themselves and to the GM. Each is equipped with a roster including the names of all possible characters in the game, their initial alignments, and their respective military strength points.

At the GM's discretion, and as a response to character development and events in the game, additional strength points may be added or existing points subtracted from one or more characters.

Female characters also contribute militarily, but in ways unique to their status. Some contribute a morale booster that doubles the strength of any militia they accompany (a militia can only be doubled in strength once, regardless of how many women accompany it).

Cockacoeske, as leader of the Pamunkey people, controls 100 military strength points. However, she can only use all these points when defending a position in Dragon Swamp. Otherwise, she can commit up to 25 strength points to an offensive action or to defending an English-designated position. Note: In the basic game, there is only the question of who controls Jamestown at the end of the game, so Cockacoeske chooses either to commit up to 25 strength points to one side or to withdraw from the Bacon-Berkeley conflict altogether and keep her 100 strength points.

Military campaigns. In the basic game, if war breaks out, the campaign is a battle for Jamestown. War is simply resolved by adding up the number of strength points that each side has amassed by the time of this battle, and victory is awarded to the faction with the most strength points. GMs may choose to add an element of uncertainty and make a final determination based on a weighted dice role.

If your instructor informs you that they will be employing the military campaign module, they will distribute supplementary materials needed to play that module.

The Smuggler

The game includes a smuggler—one character who has the power to smuggle corn (a small paper cutout of an ear of corn and marked CORN) by hiding it in the classroom if the legislature passes a law prohibiting its export.

Corn, grown by colonists and Indigenous people alike, was enormously important in Virginia as a food source for both people and livestock. Demand for tobacco, however, influenced most settlers with the necessary means to focus primarily on its production. This led to a limited food supply since colonists would choose to grow tobacco rather than food. For small-scale farmers, though, corn offered an advantageous economic pursuit. What could not be supplied by farmers and planters was procured from Indian neighbors. And demand for corn was not just local—Marylanders who similarly focused on tobacco production needed a dependable source of food, as did the inhabitants of the sugar islands in the Caribbean.

During times of intercultural warfare, corn and other food supplies became scarce. Military conflict disrupted planting and growing cycles, caused trade between Europeans and Indians to become strained or untenable, and often led to destroyed cornfields. Thus, an important consideration at the outbreak of war was the need to protect food supplies. In this game, nonexportation of corn will be debated. Preventing its export protects the colony as a whole but limits the ability of individual corn growers to market their grain to their advantage (that is, selling at the best price regardless of the location of the purchaser).

If the Grand Assembly passes a nonexportation act, all growers will be prevented from selling their corn outside the colony, effectively giving the colonial government control over the market and prices. At least one of the characters in the game has the power to smuggle corn. To do so, the smuggler must successfully hide the corn token somewhere in the classroom during each game session following passage of the nonexportation act. The smuggler must inform the GM before each session where the contraband corn is located. GMs are encouraged to determine areas that are off-limits to smuggling, such as in students' personal belongings or places that might become easily damaged in the search for the corn (such as ceiling tiles).

Anyone who discovers the contraband corn prevents the smuggler from meeting one of their victory objectives. Further, if a player successfully identifies and publicly accuses the smuggler, the accuser wins regardless of the overall outcome of the game. To do so, the accuser must inform the GM of suspicions and the reasons for them. If the GM believes the accusation is justified (but not whether or not it is correct), the game will pause and the accuser will publicly name the supposed smuggler. If the real smuggler is identified, the student playing the smuggler must admit the truth; if a student is falsely accused, the denial of the accusation should be accepted by the class (the GM, of course, can confirm the accuracy of the accusation).

If the smuggler is aligned with a particular faction when successfully accused, that faction will be docked 10 military strength points during the military campaign(s). Thus, it is not in the faction's interest to accuse one of their own members, even if the individual accuser gains a game victory.

There is no penalty for false accusations, but failure to successfully identify the smuggler precludes the accuser from making additional attempts in the future.

The Gossiper

In 1676, Virginia was awash in rumors and gossip. To simulate this, at least one character in the game has the power to spread rumors. This character will receive communications from the GM that he or she in turn must pass on to other characters in the game. Those assigned this power will win the game regardless of faction outcomes if they successfully spread rumors during the game without being discovered. Evidence of successful rumoring is public spread of the information: repetition by a third party at the podium, in a public outburst, or printed in a pamphlet that is distributed to the class.

If a player successfully identifies and publicly accuses the gossiper, the gossiper loses regardless of the overall outcome of the game while the accuser wins the game regardless of other outcomes. To make an accusation, the accuser must inform the GM of suspicions and the reasons for them. If the

GM believes the accusation is justified (but not whether or not it is correct), the game will pause and the accuser will publicly name the supposed gossiper. If the real gossiper is identified, the student must admit the truth; if a student is falsely accused, the denial of the accusation should be accepted by the class (the GM, of course, can confirm the accuracy of the accusation).

If the gossiper is aligned with a particular faction when successfully accused, that faction will be docked 10 military strength points during the military campaign(s). Thus, it is not in the faction's interest to accuse one of their own members, even if the individual accuser gains a game victory.

There is no penalty for false accusations, but failure to successfully identify the gossiper precludes the accuser from making additional attempts in the future.

Other Matters

In-Game Communication

The best way to communicate, recruit, plan, and inquire discreetly during assembly sessions is to pass notes or to use an online messaging system such as Discord or Slack. Private notes are to be treated as confidential correspondences and are an essential part of the game.

Trust the GM

The GM knows other rules beyond these listed here and may announce and enforce them. The GM also has the authority to improvise rules as necessary (in the interest of promoting successful game play and effective learning). All pronouncements from the GM are binding.

Stay in Character, Stay in the Game

The factions and characters have objectives that cannot be abandoned or changed by anyone in the game. Rather, please understand, act on, pursue, and advocate for the objectives from beginning to end. It is essential that all students immerse themselves in their roles, mastering their identities in pursuit of their characters' aims. Characters must remain in the game even if objectives are accomplished. Breaking character and intentionally neglecting objectives will be considered *abandonment* and will result in the sudden death of the character; in such cases, students will be reassigned a character.

Race and Racism

Bacon's Rebellion deals with racially charged issues, and these must be dealt with sensitively for the sake of those participating in the game. While we are inviting students to carefully explore how racism and race-based slavery developed in Virginia, and to do so in the context of intercultural and interracial frontier conflict, we are *not* asking students to engage in racist rhetoric or argumentation. The intention is not to avoid confronting such difficult issues, but to keep the game focused on the ideas that were explicitly and publicly expressed at the time. Racially charged arguments that were common in the mid-nineteenth century did not typically have a place in the public discourse of seventeenth-century Virginia (although English assumptions of the time were undergirded with racism).

For this reason, we ask that players avoid the use of racial epithets commonly associated with Africans and Native Americans. Remember that Reacting games explore ideas and ideologies. In 1676 Virginia, the English had clear ideas of racial and cultural superiority with respect to Indians, Africans, and those descended from them, but these could and were expressed in specific terms. Characters in the game who are in the position to draw distinctions between Anglo-Virginians and Native Americans should focus on cultural specifics and actions—the English are civilized because they farm, for example, while Native Americans do little more than hunt (not strictly true, but a belief of the English at the time). Regarding those arguing for and against slavery, most arguments were generally practical and economic. Although assumptions about English racial superiority lay behind the scenes, these need not be made explicit.

Staying focused on the specifics of the arguments and avoiding racial epithets helps students better learn the history without practicing racist language and playing with racial ideology. In this way the classroom may become a safe learning environment where everyone involved can better learn the nuances and complexities of Virginia's early history.

BASIC OUTLINE OF THE GAME

There are three model schedules—standard, extended, and compressed. Your instructor will inform you of which version you will be playing. The following schedule applies regardless of which version of the game is being played. For the Setup Sessions, some instructors might include more time for discussion or explaining the game mechanics, others less. This schedule is set for seventy-five-minute class periods that meet twice weekly, so some sessions may stretch over more than one class period.

In brief, the game includes the various parts (some involving more than one class session and some involving fewer):

1. Setup Session(s)
2. Social Session (soft game launch)
3. Part 1 (Legislative Session 1)
4. Part 2 (Legislative Session 2)
5. Part 3
    a. Loyalty Phase and Battle for Virginia
    b. The Future of Virginia
6. Debrief

Setup Sessions

For one or more class sessions before the game begins, as determined by the instructor, students will read and discuss the historical background found in this game book and a number of Core Texts written or delivered by the historical characters they will be playing, including some texts written by others. Students are assigned their roles and given role sheets. Instructors may lecture and familiarize players with the general background of colonial America and the status of 1676 Virginia in terms of the political, social, and economic factors leading up to Bacon's Rebellion. It is essential to complete the required reading beforehand in order to have productive sessions.

Required Readings
   Game book chapters 1–4
   Role Sheets
   Core Texts

Optional Reading
Instructors may choose to assign additional reading.

Social Session:
The Calm before the Storm

(At the end of the last Setup Session or beginning of the first game session.)

It is late February 1676, and the governor has called for a meeting of the Grand Assembly after receiving word of new raids by Native Americans along the frontier. Councillors and burgesses, summoned by the governor, have traveled down the Potomac or the Rappahannock Rivers and up the James River to Jamestown. Nearly 300 colonists have lost their lives on the frontier. The topic on the agenda for the assembly is the safety and defense of the colonists. Before the Grand Assembly convenes, however, Virginians gather in and around Jamestown to discuss the momentous events that have led to the calling of the assembly.

The following locations are designated to provide venues for private conversations, but players are not restricted to them and may move about the room as they wish, speaking to whomever they like. However, it is the prerogative of Berkeley and Bacon to exclude any indeterminate character from faction discussions until the character has made an explicit commitment to join his faction.

   Berkeley Loyalists: Green Springs Plantation
   Baconian Rebels: Drummond's Tavern, Jamestown
   Grand Assembly: Statehouse, Jamestown
   Anglo-Virginians: Lawrence's Tavern, Jamestown
   Afro-Virginians: Tower of the Old Brick Church, Jamestown

This is an opportunity for players to get to know one another and for factions to begin strategizing. Students playing characters without factions should acquaint themselves with the Berkeley Loyalists and the Bacon Dissenters to learn more about them and what they believe.

Part 1 (Legislative Session 1): "The Long Assembly," March 7, 1676

(Note: This part may comprise more than one class session.)

Safety and Defense of Virginia's Frontier

It is now March 7, 1676, and the Grand Assembly is convening. It has not met since 1660 when burgesses were last elected, giving it the name the "Long Assembly."

The governor is submitting a proposal for the safety and defense of Virginia's frontier. Several characters are scheduled to speak for or against the governor's proposal as well as other related matters.

Sergeant at arms William Drummond will call for quiet, ask members of the gallery to stand, and announce the entrance of the burgesses, councillors, and governor.

Once all are seated, the Speaker of the assembly should open the session by welcoming all present, announcing the agenda, and briefly reiterating the rules for debate. Afterward, the Speaker should call upon Sir William Berkeley first to summarize his proposal.

Anyone may speak on this matter, but the following players must address this topic with prepared speeches. It is recommended that speakers alternate between those opposed to the governor's position and those in favor. Time for questions and answers, debate, and rebuttal should follow each speech.

Welcoming address
   Col. Augustine Warner

Defensive versus offensive war strategy
   Sir William Berkeley
   Nathaniel Bacon
   Col. Philip Ludwell
   Col. John Washington
   William Drummond

Col. Edward Hill
Maj. Thomas Hansford
Maj. Isaac Allerton Jr.

Alliance with Pamunkey Indians
Col. John West
Cockacoeske
Colonel William Byrd
Edmund Chisman

Corn embargo
Col. Augustine Warner
Thomas Mathew
Francis Payne (optional)
Giles Brent
Col. Thomas Ballard

Merits of leadership: Berkeley versus Bacon
Sir Henry Chicheley
Giles Bland
Richard Lawrence

The Speaker will moderate the questioning and debate for each character. The Speaker may also pose questions and interject comments during the debate following each oral presentation. After a period of time predetermined and preannounced by the Speaker, he will call for a vote on the governor's proposal.

The assembly will consider proposals and petitions on this topic and others, time permitting. These should be delivered in writing to the GM and the Speaker of the assembly. The Speaker will order the proposals to be debated and voted upon.

Any business not completed by the end of the game session will be postponed until the next meeting. However, the game clock may be advanced between sessions, changing the historical context and possibly affecting the significance of any proposals not yet voted upon.

Subsequent Game Sessions

The dates and agendas of subsequent game sessions are shaped by decisions made in each assembly and by the advance of the game clock.

There are two more major parts to the game, possibly lasting three more class sessions, including a second legislative session, the Loyalty Phase and resolution of any military conflict, and a postconflict legislative session.

At the end or beginning of a class session, the GM may advance the clock and announce the occurrence of any significant events that took place between game sessions. Your role sheets will guide you on when to speak and what to speak about. You may also consult the GM concerning such assignments.

Debriefing

After the game ends, the instructor will conduct a debriefing session during which players have the opportunity to explain their actions without fear of repercussions. The instructor will also relate the actual historical events of the period. If the game's outcomes differed from the historical record, the class will discuss how and why. Additionally, this is a great opportunity to reflect on the gaming experience.

ASSIGNMENTS

Instructors of Reacting games have the prerogative to adjust assignments and determine grading as best fits their own classrooms. Below are recommended assignments, but students should defer to their instructor's guidelines.

Papers

All players will have written assignments detailed on their role sheets. The first paper is on the same topic as each character's assigned speech; the second is *either* a postmortem assessment of the game in which students explain the degree to which they have fulfilled their character's objectives *or* a reflection on the social and racial dynamics that were in play during the game and their takeaways (reflecting on this personally, not in character). Your instructor may allow only one of these topics. Unless otherwise specified by your instructor, these should be two to three pages long (600–900 words).

Speeches

Most players must give at least one speech; the topic and the timing are described on the role sheet. Generally, speeches should be at least three minutes but no more than five minutes long. Again, these requirements are contingent on the instructor's expectations for the class.

Grades

Instructors are responsible for informing students beforehand how the various elements of this game correspond to the course's grading scheme. There are several potential elements that may be considered: writing assignment(s), in-class participation, speeches, and game/victory points. The instructor must make clear whether game/victory points will count toward the overall grade in the class.

COUNTERFACTUALS

To facilitate the smooth operation of this game and to open debate on some key ideas that might otherwise be overlooked, the authors have manipulated a few elements of the history of Bacon's Rebellion and Virginia.

First, the political situation and processes are simplified. Each session of the Grand Assembly may have lasted for hours and even days. Even though the main issues were deliberated, minor and insignificant issues were also handled. Furthermore, processes for order and tradition took longer than this game can afford. Though such things may be valuable to gain the full experience of the Grand Assembly, for purposes of meeting the learning objectives in a reasonable time, the game only deals with a few key issues. Due to sheer numbers, not every county can be represented in the Grand Assembly, and the decision-making and governance processes have been simplified by conflating the work of the burgesses and the councillors into a single legislative body. Furthermore, political alignments have been modified or presumed to create the necessary dynamics for gameplay.

Second, the timing of various events is condensed and somewhat altered but does not dramatically distort the meaning of historical events. While each event influencing the game actually occurred, some incidents during the period will be out of chronological order and may follow a more compressed chronology. These slight alterations discourage re-enactments by improving game flow and allowing students to react instead.

Lastly, most of the characters reflect real individuals based on historical research, but some characters are either fictional composites or based in history but brought into the game without evidence of their involvement in the conflict. In the historical scholarship, individual people of color are not recorded as participants, but documents of the era recorded the number of people of color who participated. To aid in the discussion of critical issues prior to the rebellion and in its aftermath—especially pertaining to matters of women, enslaved people, and laborers—we have created characters who did exist but may not have been participants during this period. They represent those who have gone historically unnamed and unrecognized. Thus, enslaved people, free laborers, and indentured servants should not be seen in this game as strictly historically relevant individuals with respect to Bacon's Rebellion, but they should be viewed as representatives of dozens or more Virginians who shared the same plight.

These counterfactuals condense the game rather than change history, allowing you to consider, evaluate, and debate, in a few hours, issues that emerged and were decided on over the course of weeks and months. These alterations also create both an urgency and a contingency around what is decided and reacted to in class. The most significant counterfactual is the course itself and the outcome of the game. The game structure is designed to prevent players from pursuing unlikely historical outcomes, but this still allows room for possible but counterfactual endings. The history is now yours to create.

Live it, breathe it, react to it!

4

Roles and Factions

Every character in this game represents a person who lived in Virginia during the time of Bacon's Rebellion, played a role in it, or both. The instructor will make the role assignments and deliver the role sheets prior to the first game session. Your role sheet is a confidential document—it cannot be safely shared with any other player (some of whom have secret motives and interests of their own). Learn your role well and stick to it. The game is played "in character," meaning that you can share certain elements of your role sheet only by articulating and explaining from your character's perspective. In other words, you speak and react as your character and according to your role but use contemporary language to do so.

The Berkeleyan Faction

The Berkeleyan Faction supports Sir William Berkeley and is a staunch defender of his governance. It is committed to the established order and will take up arms when called upon by the governor. Most members are very wealthy planters, with their plantations and estates in or near Jamestown, and they are opposed to raiding Native American tribes mostly due to their own economic interests in the Indian trade. As members of the elite class, they owe their position to Berkeley as much as to any other cause.

Sir William Berkeley. Governor. Sir Berkeley has served as governor of Virginia from 1641–52 and from 1660 to the present, the longest-serving governor of Virginia. Well after completing his education at Oxford University, Berkeley's political career in England culminated in receiving his knighthood by King Charles I. Currently, his primary concerns are diversifying the tobacco-based economy and securing peace and trade agreements with neighboring Native American tribes.

Col. Philip Ludwell. Councillor. Ludwell immigrated to Virginia, becoming a planter at a sizable plantation called Rich Neck in the Middle Plantation community of James City County. He and his older brother Thomas (who is currently visiting England) are the newest members of the council of state along with Nathaniel Bacon. A relative of the governor, Philip has also become a close friend of the Berkeleys.

Col. John West II. Burgess. A Virginia native and son of a former governor of Virginia, West resides in West Point and has served as commander of the New Kent County Militia for over twenty-five years. With decades of militia experience, his presence and command in a conflict is invaluable. Rumor has it that his dealings with Native Americans have led him into a special relationship with the chief of the Pamunkey. Nevertheless, West is a member of the House of Burgesses for New Kent County.

Lady Frances Culpeper Stephens Berkeley. Free Anglo-Virginian woman. Born as Frances Culpeper, her father was a member of the Virginia Company of London. After the death of her first husband, she received absolute possession of a 1,350-acre plantation in Warwick County called Boldrup. A widow with valuable and substantial property, she is now married to Sir William Berkeley, which has increased her prestige while allying the governor with the Culpeper family, including her cousins, the Bacons. She is politically influential and an outspoken supporter of her husband's government.

Sir Henry Chicheley. Lieutenant governor. Born in Wimpole, England, Chicheley is from a wealthy family and was educated at Oxford University. A staunch royalist and military commander, Chicheley was knighted by King Charles I before the king's execution. Finding refuge in Lancaster County, Chicheley married into Virginia's gentry and became a supporter of Berkeley's administration. Chicheley currently serves Virginia as the lieutenant governor.

Maj. Robert Beverley. Burgess. An immigrant from Yorkshire, England, Beverley came to Virginia and settled in Middlesex County. Beverley owns over 28,000 acres in four counties, which he amassed through marriage to a wealthy widow. He is a major exporter of tobacco and importer of various manufactured goods. In addition to serving as a major in the Middlesex County militia, he serves in the House of Burgesses and has recently been appointed as acting attorney general of Virginia by his good friend, Governor Berkeley.

Col. Nicholas Spencer. Councillor. After immigrating to Westmoreland County to serve as an agent overseeing the investment of his cousins, the Culpeper family, Spencer secured an appointment as a customs collector on the Potomac where he works closely with Col. John Washington. As cousin to Lady Berkeley, Spencer was appointed by the governor to the council and made president of that body. Spencer owns James Revel, an indentured servant.

Maj. Isaac Allerton Jr. Burgess. A descendant of Mayflower "Pilgrims," Allerton was educated at Harvard College and is now a planter in Northumberland County. Prior to acquiring over 5,000 acres of land along the Rappahannock River, Allerton served as an officer in the Westmoreland County militia. While formerly representing Westmoreland County in the House of Burgesses, Allerton currently represents Northumberland County where the majority of his land lies.

The Baconian Faction

The Baconian Faction supports Nathaniel Bacon, and many of its members are unsatisfied by the action and inaction of the governor and assembly. Aware of increasing violence and rumors of more raids, murders, and tortures along the frontier by Native Americans, they believe that immediate action is necessary and overdue, and Nathaniel Bacon is the one to bring about change. He lives on the frontier, has experienced Native American attacks himself, and has a seat on the council of state and a family relationship to the governor's wife. Each Baconite has had personal dealings with Sir Berkeley and lacks confidence in his leadership or holds a grudge against him. Members therefore support Bacon and most are committed to an offensive military strategy in the conflict with Virginia's Native neighbors.

Nathaniel Bacon. Councillor. A resident of Henrico County since 1674, Bacon was appointed to the council on the strength of his family relations. Recently his farm has been attacked by Susquehannocks, and he clashes with Berkeley by advocating a more offensive approach to the Indian problem.

William Drummond. Freeholder. An immigrant from Scotland, Drummond rose from an indentured servant to the first governor of the emerging colony on the Albemarle Sound (North Carolina). After many clashes with Governor Berkeley, Drummond has been seen commiserating with his drinking buddies Nathaniel Bacon and Richard Lawrence. Nevertheless, Drummond is now the sergeant at arms of the Grand Assembly.

Col. William Byrd. Freeholder. A recent immigrant, Byrd inherited the estate of his uncle, a wealthy planter in Henrico County. Byrd soon extended his residence, wealth, and political power. Upon the arrival of Bacon, Byrd became a neighbor, fellow militia officer, and drinking companion. He is also a partner with Bacon in the Indian trade, bringing both into direct competition with Berkeley and his followers who seek to control that trade for themselves.

Giles Bland. Freeholder. A recent immigrant from London, England, Bland arrived in Virginia to assume his duties as a customs collector. However, after the death of his uncle Theodorick Bland, who had managed the family's Virginia property, he came into conflict with his aunt, Anna Bennett Bland, over control of the estate. But Aunt Anna's friends include Governor Berkeley, putting her nephew outside the governor's circle. Somewhat of a free spirit and possessing a sharp tongue, Giles has had numerous confrontations with the governor and the council that have led to his suspension as customs collector (although this has not prevented him from continuing to collect duties).

Richard Lawrence. Burgess. A relative newcomer to Virginia, Lawrence was born in England and educated at Oxford University, hence his nickname "The Scholar." Though not a soldier or planter, Lawrence became a businessman and housekeeper of Jamestown property frequented by Drummond and Bacon when they are in town. It is clear to Lawrence and many of the other highborn newcomers to Virginia that Governor Berkeley is more interested in centralizing power in the hands of himself and his select friends than sharing it with those of social standing and education.

Maj. Thomas Hansford. Freeholder. A Virginia native born in York County, Hanford is an owner of a small plantation in York County. He also serves as an officer in the county militia and has aspirations of higher leadership. An outspoken proponent of an offensive approach to the current conflict, Hansford is ready to take up arms.

Indeterminates

Indeterminates are not members of any faction at the beginning of the game, nor do they function as a faction. On the contrary, they may well have divergent views and opinions. Indeterminates can join a faction at any time and alter the outcome of the game greatly.

Col. John Washington. Burgess. Washington became a merchant in London, investing in a merchant ship engaged in the tobacco trade from the colonies. He eventually settled in Virginia where he married Anne Pope and received 700 acres on Mattox Creek in Westmoreland County of the Northern Neck. A successful planter, Washington relies on enslaved labor and indentured servants, and he also serves as a burgess for Westmoreland County and a colonel in the Virginia militia.

Cockacoeske. Native American. Also known as the "Queen of the Pamunkey," Cockacoeske became a Pamunkey (Powhatan) chief after the death of her husband, Totopotomo. Since the Treaty of 1646, the Pamunkey have been tributaries to the English Crown. Sir Berkeley has had trade and military relationships with the Pamunkey, but many Pamunkeys have been caught in the crossfire of intercultural warfare.

Col. Augustine Warner Jr. Burgess and Speaker of the assembly. A Virginia native, Warner is the only son to the early Virginia settlers who patented a plantation called "Austin's Desire" in Gloucester County. Warner was educated in London, became a prominent planter and landowner, and was elected to the House of Burgesses representing Gloucester County. He has recently been selected by Governor Berkeley as the Speaker of the assembly of Virginia.

Thomas Mathew. Freeholder. A merchant and planter in Stafford County. With his farm on the frontier, Mathew has always had issues with his Native

American "neighbors," but some now blame the current troubles on his underhanded dealings with the Doegs. Although Mathew is not interested in pursuing politics, some of his influential friends have encouraged him to run in the next election for burgesses.

Arthur Allen. Freeholder. Son of a wealthy tobacco merchant and educated in England, Allen inherited one of the largest plantations in Surry County and along with it, his father's pride and joy—a three-story home called Allen's Brick House. He has increased his holdings to almost 10,000 acres in Surry and the Isle of Wight counties. Like some of his fellow planters, Allen is beginning to shift his workforce from temporary indentured servants to permanently enslaved Africans.

Francis Payne. Free Afro-Virginian. A former enslaved African on the Eastern Shore, Payne is now a free man of color and a successful planter. Although a planter and landowner, he is not a freeholder. Nevertheless, he is well known for utilizing his social status to gain victory in the courts. Payne currently resides at his plantation in Northampton County.

Col. Thomas Godwin. Freeholder. A former indentured servant, Godwin partnered with another former indentured servant to patent land in York County and became a successful planter. He also purchased a tract in Chuckatuck parish in the recently formed Isle of Wight County. He has represented Nansemond County in the House of Burgesses in the past, but as of March 1676, he is not serving as a burgess.

John Punch. Enslaved Afro-Virginian. Born in Angola, Punch was kidnapped, involuntarily transported to America, and sold to Hugh Gwyn. Although he apparently had a limited term of servitude, at about age twenty Punch ran away with two white indentured servants. All were captured and all received the punishment of thirty lashes, but while the Anglo-Virginians received just four-year additions to their terms of service, Punch's term was converted to slavery for life.

James Revel. Indentured Anglo-Virginian. Revel left England as an indentured servant and landed in Rappahannock County, where he is serving an extraordinarily long term in exchange for his passage and dreaming of gaining the prosperity of his master, Col. Nicholas Spencer Jr. While his indenture is over soon, he is deeply concerned about his future prospects and the safety of Virginia's frontier, the only place that has available land to newly released servants.

Sarah Grendon. Free Anglo-Virginian woman. A native Virginian and a widow of the late councillor Thomas Stegge Jr., she is currently married to Lt. Col. Thomas Grendon Jr. of the Charles City County militia. Grendon lives in the parish of Westover in Charles City County, and her husband has vast estates in Virginia and in England. As a merchant, her husband is currently in England overseeing his holdings there. She is the aunt of William Byrd and is known to frequent Lawrence Tavern in Jamestown.

Maj. Edmund Chisman Jr. Freeholder. A Virginia native, Edmund Chisman was born and raised in York County. After marrying a woman named Lydia, Chisman acquired 200 acres of land in York County and became a justice of the peace. Eventually he became a major in the York County militia. Chisman's father marched against the Pamunkey Indians in 1644, and Chisman greatly respects and honors his father's memory.

Capt. Giles Brent. Freeholder. Born of Native American, English, and Catholic heritage, Brent became a prosperous young planter and militia captain after inheriting an extensive estate when his father, a prominent militia officer himself, died. Having the advantage of learning a Native American language from his mother, who was an orphan daughter of a Piscataway Indian leader, Brent has become invaluable in the current crisis. Even though Brent is half Native American, he yearns for full acceptance as an Anglo-Virginian.

Col. Thomas Ballard. Councillor. A native Virginian born in Warwick County, Ballard started his political career as the clerk of York County where he owned land. He also owned land in Gloucester County and spent most of his adult life buying and selling property for profit, even selling land to Nathaniel Bacon. After serving in the House of

Burgesses representing James City County, he became a close associate with the governor who, in turn, appointed him to the council. Recently, Ballard purchased a 330-acre farm in Middle Plantation where he resides with his wife, Anna.

Elizabeth Key Grinstead ("Black Bess"). Free Afro-Virginian woman. Born to an enslaved woman and fathered by the late Thomas Key—"an ancient planter" and member of the House of Burgesses who had land on Warwicksqueake River—Grinstead petitioned for freedom in Northumberland County and won. However, the decision was overturned by a higher court. Her lawyer, William Grinstead, eventually won her freedom by marrying her, fathering two of her children, and bringing her case to the General Assembly. Since his death, Grinstead's freedom and the status of her children are at risk because of the recent discriminatory laws passed by the Grand Assembly.

Emanuel Driggus. Free Afro-Virginian man. Born to enslaved African parents, Driggus has lived all his adult life in Virginia. As a young man, he ran away but was recaptured and had his term extended. Eventually, however, he received his freedom after the death of his master. Relatively successful as a free Afro-Virginian, Driggus seeks the freedom of his two daughters, who remain enslaved.

Col. Edward Hill II. Burgess. Born in Virginia to a wealthy planter family, Hill purchased the Shirley Plantation and became the master of his father's extensive landholdings upon his death. Like his father, Hill served as colonel of the Charles City County militia and is currently representing the county in the House of Burgesses.

5
Core Texts

NOTE ON THE TEXTS

In order to play the game well, one must have a grasp of the documents that follow. Please keep the chronology in mind; many of these sources originated years or decades before the events of 1675–76, but they help establish the social, legal, and racial context of pre-Bacon's Rebellion Virginia. Others were composed during and even after Bacon's Rebellion but are included here because of the paucity of documents contemporary to the rebellion itself. Yet many are based on memories of the events by first-hand observers and participants and are necessary for gameplay. Other texts are provided for further context but are not meant to encourage a reenactment of the past. Instead, they may be used to inform possible arguments to persuade others and to inspire your own writings, speeches, and arguments based on your character and objectives outlined in the role sheets. Please note that many of the documents have been silently modernized in spelling and punctuation to ease understanding and interpretation.

In some cases, portions of the original source have been omitted as represented by an ellipsis. Bracketed material was added by various editors of the source material; additions in italics were added by the game authors.

John Rolfe, on the Arrival of African Slaves (1619)

The first African slaves arrived at Jamestown in 1619, introducing race-based slavery to the colony. Slavery was not unknown to the English, and it was part of the Atlantic world of which English colonization was a part, but the English did not actively introduce the institution in Virginia. Instead, its introduction was incidental to the development of the colony, although it would become instrumental in shaping Virginia's society and economy and in turn the rest of the southern colonies (and later states). This report by John Rolfe notes the arrival of each ship at Jamestown and highlights a number of newsworthy events and various concerns about the management of the colony, but he mentions the arrival and purchase of the enslaved Africans matter-of-factly. Of historical significance is the arrival of Governor George Yearley and notice of his intent to institute a House of Burgesses. Thus the arrival of enslaved Africans and the establishment of a representative government coincided during this year in Virginia.

What concerns are expressed regarding provisions, labor, and agricultural production?

What observations does the author make of the arrival of Africans? Of the treatment of English servants? How do these compare?

What insights can you glean regarding Indian relations?

Source: John Smith, *Works, 1608–1631*, pt. 2, ed. Edward Arber (Westminster, UK: Archibald Constable, 1895), 540–43.

A relation from Master John Rolfe. . . .

For to begin with the year of our Lord, 1619. there arrived a little pinnace privately from England about Easter [Easter Sunday O.S. was 28 Mar. in 1619] for Captain Argall; who taking order for his affairs, within four or five days returned in her, and left for his Deputy, Captain Nathaniel Powell.

On the eighteenth of April, which was but ten or twelve days after, arrived Sir George Yearley [*the new governor*], by whom we understood Sir Edwin Sandys was chosen Treasurer [*of the Virginia Company*], and Master John Farrar his Deputy; and what great supplies was a preparing to be sent us, which did ravish us so much with joy and content, we thought ourselves now fully satisfied for our long toil and labors, and as happy men as any in the world. . . .

Sir George Yearly to begin his government, added to be of his council, Captain Francis West, Captain Nathaniel Powell, Master John Pory, Master John Rolfe, and Master William Wickham, and Master Samuel Macocke, and propounded to have a general assembly [*House of Burgesses*] with all expedition.

Upon the twelfth of this Month [April 1619], came in a pinnace of Captain Bargraves; and on the seventeenth Captain Lownes, and one Master Evans, who intended to plant themselves at Waraskoyak: but now Ophechankanough will not come at us, that causes us to suspect his former promises.

In May came in the *Margaret of Bristol*, with four and thirty men, all well and in health; and also many devout gifts: and we were much troubled in examining some scandalous letters sent into England, to disgrace this Country with barrenness, to discourage the adventurers [*investors in the Virginia Company*], and so bring it and us to ruin and confusion. Notwithstanding, we find by them of best experience, an industrious man not other ways employed, may well tend four acres of Corn, and 1000 plants of Tobacco; and where they say an acre will yield but three or four barrels, we have ordinarily four or five, but of new ground six, seven, and eight, and a barrel of Peas and Beans, which we esteem as good as two of Corn, which is after thirty or forty bushels an acre, so that one man may provide Corn for five; and apparel for two by the profit of his Tobacco. They say also English Wheat will yield but sixteen bushels an acre, and we have reaped thirty: besides to manure the Land, no place hath more white and blew Marble than here, had we but Carpenters to build and make Carts and Plows, and skillful men that know how to use them, and train up our cattle to draw them; which though we endeavor to effect, yet our want of experience brings but little to perfection but planting Tobacco. And yet of that, many are so covetous to have much, they make little good; besides there are so many sophisticating Tobacco-mongers in England, were it never so bad, they would sell it for Verinas, and the trash that remaineth should be Virginia: such devilish bad minds we know some of our own Country-men do bear, not only to the business, but also to our mother England herself; could they or durst they as freely defame her.

The 25th of June came in the *Trial* with Corn and Cattle all in safety, which took from us clearly all fear of famine; then our governor and council caused Burgesses to be chosen in all places, and met at a general Assembly, where all matters were debated [that were] thought expedient for the good of the Colony, and Captain Ward was sent to Monahigan in New England, to fish in May, and returned the latter end of May, but to small purpose, for they wanted Salt. The *George* also was sent to New-found-land with the Cape Merchant: there she bought fish, that defrayed her charges, and made a good voyage in seven weeks.

About the last of August came in a Dutch man-of-war that sold us twenty Negars.[1] And Lapazaus King of Patawomeck, came to Jamestown, to desire two ships to come trade in his River, for a more plentiful year of Corn had not been in a long time, yet very contagious, and by the treachery of one Poule, in a manner turned heathen, we were very jealous the Savages would surprise us.

The Governors *[that is, directors of the Virginia Company]* have bounded four Corporations; which is the Companies, the University, the Governors, and Glebe land: Ensigne Wil. Spencer, and Thomas Barret a Sergeant, with some others of the ancient Planters being set free, were the first farmers that went forth; and have chosen places to their content: so that now knowing their own land, they strive who should exceed in building and planting. . . .

Notwithstanding the ill rumors of the unwholesomeness of Jamestown, the newcomers that were planted at old Paspaheghe, [a] little more than a mile from it, had their healths better than any in the Country.

In December, Captain War returned from Patawomeck, the people there dealt falsely with him, so that he took 800 bushels of Corn from them perforce. . . .

Now you are to understand, that because there have been many complaints against the Governors, Captains, and Officers in Virginia: for buying and selling [English] men and boys, or to be set over from one to another for a yearly rent, was held in England a thing most intolerable; or that the tenants or lawful servants should be put from their places, or abridged their Covenants, was so odious, that the very report thereof brought a great scandal to the general action. The council in England did send many good and worthy instructions for the amending [of] those abuses, and appointed a hundred men should at the Companies charge be allotted and provided to serve and attend the Governor during the time of his government, which number he was to make good at his departure, and leave to his Successor in like manner; fifty to the Deputy-Governor of the College land, and fifty to the Deputy of the Companies land, fifty to the Treasurer, to the Secretary five and twenty, and more to the Marshall and Cape merchant; which they are also to leave to their successors; and likewise to every particular Officer such a competency, as he might live well in his Office, without oppressing any under their charge: which good law I pray God it be well observed, and then we may truly say in Virginia, we are the most happy people in the world.

Virginia Laws Regarding Labor, Slavery, and Race (1619–1676)

These excerpts from the law books of colonial Virginia provide a glimpse into the evolution of racism and slavery from 1619 until 1676.

Legal and court records pose special challenges to historians. As you read the source, look for the subtleties.

For court cases, ask who is being tried. What is the nature of the crime? How does the crime relate to the interaction between races? How is justice applied differently depending on the racial classification of the defendant? How does the administration of justice change over time?

When laws are established, ask what the stated intent of the law is. What does the law reveal about efforts to control and maintain an effective source of labor? How do the laws implement racial distinctions? When are racial distinctions ignored? How do the laws change over time with respect to racial concerns?

Finally, make note of the distinctions within the laws between Native Americans and Afro-Virginians in terms of service and the qualifying effect of Christianity on individuals from each group.

Source: William Waller Hening, ed., *The Statutes at Large; Being a Collection of the Laws of Virginia, From the First Session of the Legislature, in the Year 1619* (New York: R&W&G Bartow, 1823), 1:146, 226, 455–56, 551–52; 2:116–17, 170, 260, 270, 280–81, 283, 288.

From the Minutes of the Judicial Proceedings of the Governor and Council of Virginia:

September 17th, 1630. Hugh Davis [*English*] to be soundly whipped, before an assembly of Negroes and others for abusing himself to the dishonor of God and shame of Christians, by defiling his body in lying with a negro; which fault he is to acknowledge next Sabbath day.

Extracts from the Minutes of the Proceedings of the Governor and Council of Virginia:

1640
Robert Sweet to do penance in church according to laws of England, for getting a negroe woman with child, and the woman whipped.

At a Grand Assembly, 6th January, 1639—Sr. Francis Wyatt, Gov.:

Act X
All persons except negroes to be provided with arms and ammunition or be fined at pleasure of the Governor and Council.

At a Grand Assembly held at James City, March 13th, 1657–58:

Act XLVIII
It is enacted that in case any Indian do dispose of his child to any person or persons whatsoever, either for education or instruction in Christian religion, or for learning the English tongue or for what cause soever, those persons to whom such child shall be disposed shall not assign or transfer such Indian child to any other whatsoever, upon any pretense whatsoever of right to him or any time of service due from him. And it is further enacted that such Indian child shall be free and at his own disposal at the age of twenty five years.

At a Grand Assembly held at James City March the 23d 1661–62:

Act CII
Whereas there are diverse loitering runaways in this country who very often absent themselves from their masters' service and sometimes in a long time cannot be found, that loss of the time and the charge in the seeking them often exceeding the value of their labor: Be it therefore enacted that all runaways that shall absent themselves from their said masters service, shall be liable to make satisfaction by service after the times by custom or indenture is expired. Namely, double their times of service so neglected, and if the time of their running away was in the crop or the charge of recovering them extraordinary the court

58 CORE TEXTS

shall limit a longer time of service proportionable to the damage the master shall make appear he hath sustained, and because the adjudging the time they should serve is often referred until the time by indenture is expired, when the proof of what is due is very uncertain, it is enacted that the master of any runaway that intends to take the benefit of this act, shall as soon as he has recovered him carry him to the next commissioner and there declare and prove the time of his absence, and the charge he has been at in his recovery, which commissioner thereupon shall grant his certificate, and the court on that certificate pass judgment for the time he shall serve for his absence; and in case any English servant shall run away in company of any negroes who are incapable of making satisfaction by addition of a time, it is enacted that the English so running away in the company with them shall at the time of service to their own masters expired, serve the masters of the said negroes for their absence so long as they should have done by this act if they had not been slaves, every Christian in company serving his proportion; and if the negroes be lost or die in such time of their being run away, the Christian servants in company with them shall by proportion among them, either pay four thousand five hundred pounds of tobacco and cask or four years' service for every negroe so lost or dead.

At a Grand Assembly held at James City . . . from the twentie third of March 1660 . . . and thence to the twentie third of December 1662:

Act XII

Whereas some doubts have arisen whether children got by any Englishman upon a negro woman should be slave or free, be it therefore enacted and declared by this present grand assembly, that all children borne in this country shall be held bond or free only according to the condition of the mother, And that if any Christian shall commit fornication with a negro man or woman, he or she so offending shall pay double the fines imposed by the former act.

At a Grand Assembly held at James City the twenty third day of September 1667:

Act III

Whereas some doubts have risen whether children that are slaves by birth, and by the charity and piety of their owners made partakers of the blessed sacrament of baptism, should by virtue of their baptism be made free; It is enacted and declared by this grand assembly, and the authority thereof, that the conferring of baptism does not alter the condition of the person as to his bondage or freedom; that diverse masters, freed from this doubt, may more carefully endeavor the propagation of Christianity by permitting children, though slaves, or those of greater growth if capable to be admitted to that sacrament.

At a Grand Assembly held at James City . . . from the 23rd September, 1667, to the seventeenth of September 1668:

Act VII

Whereas some doubts have arisen whether negro women set free were still to be accounted tithable according to the former act, It is declared by this grand assembly that negro women, though permitted to enjoy their freedom yet ought not in all respects to be admitted to a full fruition of the exemptions and impunities of England, and are still liable to payment of taxes.

At a Grand Assembly held at James City . . . from the seventeenth of September, 1668, to the twentieth of October 1669:

Act I

Whereas the only law in force for the punishment of refractory servants resisting their master, mistress, or overseer cannot be inflicted upon negroes, nor the obstinacy of many of them by other then violent means suppressed, be it enacted and declared by this grand assembly, if any slave resist his master (or other by his masters order correcting him) and by the extremity of the correction should chance to die, that his death shall not be accounted felony, but the master (or that other person appointed by the master to punish him) be acquitted from molestation, since it cannot be presumed that prepensed malice (which alone makes murder felony) should induce any man to destroy his own estate.

At a Grand Assembly held at James City . . . from the twentieth of October 1669 to the third of October 1670:

Act V
Whereas it has been questioned whether Indians or negroes manumitted, or otherwise free, could be capable of purchasing Christian servants. It is enacted that no negro or Indian though baptised and enjoying their own freedom shall be capable of any such purchase of Christians, but yet not debarred from buying any of their own nation.

Act XII
Whereas some dispute have arisen whither Indians taken in wart by any other nation, and by that nation that taketh them sold to the English, are servants for life or term of years, It is resolved and enacted that all servants not being Christians imported into this colony by shipping shall be slaves for their lives; but what shall come by land shall serve, if boys or girls, until thirty years of age, if men or women twelve years and no longer.

At a Grand Assembly held at James City . . . from the third of October 1670 to the 20th of September, 1671:

Act IV
Whereas in the former act concerning the estates of persons dying intestate, it is provided that sheep, horses, and cattle should be delivered in kind to the orphan, when they came of age, according to the several ages the said cattle were of when the guardian took them into his possession, to which some have desired that negroes may be added; this assembly considering the difficulty of procuring negroes in kind as also the value and hazard of their lives have doubted whether any sufficient men would be found who would engage themselves to deliver negroes of equal ages if the specific negroes should die, or become by age or accident unserviceable; Be it therefore enacted and ordained by this grand assembly and the authority thereof that the consideration of this be referred to the county courts who are hereby authorized and empowered either to cause such negroes to be duly apprised, sold at an outcry, or preserved in kind, as they then find it most expedient for preservation, improvement or advancement of the estate and interest of such orphans.

Anthony Johnson, A Former Slave Claims His Slave Property (1655)

Perhaps no case so succinctly demonstrates the fluidity of race and class in mid-seventeenth-century Virginia as the legal battle between Anthony Johnson, Robert Parker, and John Casor. Casor, of African descent, claimed he had served his term of indenture to Anthony Johnson, also of African descent, and was seeking refuge and help from Englishman Robert Parker. The court ruled in Johnson's favor, agreeing that Casor was a slave for life. But they did so on the strength of third-party testimony—that of Samuel Gouldsmith (rendered Goldsmith in this document), a local English planter who effectively served as Johnson's patron.

Consider how political alignments might emerge given socioeconomic structures in which lesser planters such as Johnson benefit from the power and influence of more significant planters such as Gouldsmith. Is Johnson free to vote for whomever he likes? What does he owe Gouldsmith? And where do Casor's sympathies lie? To what degree are racial alignments challenged and transcended by these patron-client relationships?

Source: Warren M. Billings, ed., *The Old Dominion in the Seventeenth Century: A Documentary History of Virginia, 1660–1689*, rev. ed. (Chapel Hill: University of North Carolina Press for the Omohundro Institute of Early American History and Culture, 2007), 180–81.

The deposition of Captain Samuel Goldsmith taken (in open court) 8th of March Says, That being at the house of Anthony Johnson Negro (about the beginning of November last to receive a hogshead of tobacco) a Negro called John Cas[o]r came to this Deponent, and told him that he came into Virginia for seven or Eight years (per Indenture) And that he had demanded his freedom of his master Anthony Johnson; And further said that Johnson had kept him his servant seven years longer than he ought, And desired that this deponent would see that he might have no wrong, whereupon your Deponent demanded of Anthony Johnson his Indenture, he answered, he never saw any; The said Negro (John Casor) replied, he came for a certain time and had an Indenture Anthony Johnson said he never did see any But that he had him for his life; Further this deponent said That mr. Robert Parker and George Parker they knew that the said Negro had an Indenture (in on Mr. Carye hundred on the other side of the Bay) And the said Anthony Johnson did not tell the negro go free The said John Casor would recover most of his Cows of him; Then Anthony Johnson (as this deponent did suppose) was in a fear. Upon this his Son in law, his wife and his 2 sons persuaded the said Anthony Johnson to set the said John Casor free. more saith not.

    Samuel Goldsmith

This day Anthony Johnson Negro made his complaint to the Court against mr. Robert Parker and declared that he detained his servant John Casor negro (under pretence that the said Negro is a free man). The Court seriously considering and maturely weighing the premises, do find that the said Mr. Robert Parker most unjustly kept the said Negro from Anthony Johnson his master as appears by the deposition of Captain Samuel Goldsmith and many probable circumstances. It is therefore the Judgement of the Court and ordered That the said John Casor Negro forthwith return unto the service of his said master Anthony Johnson, And that mr. Robert Parker make payment of all charges in the suit, also Execution.

The Case of Elizabeth Key (1655–1656)

The following excerpts relate to the fascinating case of Elizabeth Key Grinstead—a character in this game. Hers is one of the earliest cases of a person of African descent suing—successfully—for her freedom (and that of her son). She then married Englishman John Grinstead after he finished his term of indenture. Her case expands on the nuances of the intersection of race and class previously introduced in the Anthony Johnson case, adding gender to the mix.

Who is the father of Elizabeth? Of Elizabeth's children? How is Elizabeth's status established? Who gives testimony? How does this case seem to relate to the laws listed earlier? (Pay attention to the chronology.)

Source: Warren M. Billings, ed., *The Old Dominion in the Seventeenth Century: A Documentary History of Virginia, 1660–1689*, rev. ed. (Chapel Hill: University of North Carolina Press for the Omohundro Institute of Early American History and Culture, 2007), 195–99.

The Court doth order that Col. Thomas Speke one of the overseers of the Estate of Col. John Mottram deceased shall have an Appeal to the Quarter Court next at James City in a Cause depending between the said overseers and Elizabeth a Moletto he the said Col. Speke giving such caution as to Law doth belong.

We whose names are underwritten being impaneled upon a Jury to try a difference between Elizabeth pretended Slave to the Estate of Col. John Mottrom deceased and the overseers of the said Estate do find that the said Elizabeth ought to be free as by several oaths might appear which we desire might be Recorded and that the charges of Court be paid out of the said Estate. [names of the jury omitted]

Memorandum it is Conditioned and agreed by and betwixt Thomas Key on the one part and Humphrey Higginson on the other part [word missed] that the said Thomas Key hath put unto the said Humphrey one Negro Girl by name Elizabeth for the during [term?] of nine years after the date hereof provided that the [said?] Humphrey do find and allow the said

CORE TEXTS 61

Elizabeth meat drink [and?] apparel during the said term And also the said Thomas Key that if the said Humphrey do die before the end of the said time above specified that then the said girl be free from the said Humphrey Higginson and his assigns Also if he said Humphrey Higgenson do go for England with an Intention to live and remain there that then he shall carry the said Girl with him and to pay for her passage and likewise that he put not off said Girl to any man but to keep her himself In witness whereof I the said Humphrey Higginson. Sealed and delivered in the presence of us
  Robert Booth Francis Miryman.
  20th January 1655 this writing was Recorded.

Mr. Nicholas Jurnew aged 53 years or thereabouts sworn and Examined Saith That about 16 or 17 years past this deponent heard a flying report at York that Elizabeth a Negro Servant to the Estate of Col. John Mottrom deceased was the Child of Mr. Key but the said Mr. Key said that a Turke of Capt. Mathewes was Father to the Girl and further this deponent saith not.
  signed Nicholas Jumew
  20th January 1655 Jurat in Curia ["sworn in court"]

Anthony Lenton aged 41 years or thereabouts sworn and Examined Saith that about 19 years past this deponent was a servant to Mr. Humphrey Higginson and at that time one Elizabeth a Molletto now servant to the Estate of Col. John Mottrom deceased was then a servant to the said mr. Higginson and as the Neighbours reported was bought of mr. Higginson with the said servant both himself and his Wife intended a voyage for England and at the nine years end (as the Neighbours reported) the said Mr. Higginson was bound to carry the said servant for England unto the said mr. Key, but before the said mr. Key went his Voyage he Died about Kecotan, and as the Neighbours reported the said mr. Higginson said at the nine years end he would carry the said Molletto for England and give her a portion and let her shift for herself And it was a Common report amongst the Neighbours that the said Molletto was mr. Key's Child begot by him and further this deponent saith not.
  the mark of Anthony Lenton
  20th January 1655 Jurat in Curia

Mrs. Elizabeth Newman aged 80 years or thereabouts sworn and examined Saith that it was a common Fame in Virginia that Elizabeth a Molletto now servant to the Estate of Col. John Mottrom deceased was the Daughter of mr. Key; and the said Key was brought to Blunt-point Court and there fined for getting his Negroe woman with Child which said Negroe was the Mother of the said Molletto and the said fine was for getting the Negroe with Child which Child was the said Elizabeth and further this deponent saith not.
  the mark of Elizabeth Newman
  20th January 1655 Jurat in Curia

John Bayles aged 33 years or thereabouts sworn and Examined Saith that at the House of Col. John Mattrom Black Besse was termed to be mr. Key's Bastard and John Key calling her Black Bess mrs. Speke Checked him and said Sirra you must call her Sister for she is your Sister and the said John Key did call her Sister and further this deponent Saith not.
  the mark of John Bayles
  20th January 1655 Jurat in Curia

The deposition of Alice Larrett aged 38 years or thereabouts Sworn and Examined Saith that Elizabeth which is at Col. Mottroms is twenty five years of age or thereabouts and that I saw her mother go to bed to her Master many times and I heard her mother Say that she was mr. Key's daughter and further Saith not.
  the mark of Alice Larrett Sworn before mr. Nicholas Morris 19th Jan. 1655.
  20th January this deposition was Recorded

Anne Clark aged 39 or thereabouts Sworn and Examined Saith that she this deponent was present when a Condition was made between mr. Humphrey Higginson and mr. Key for a servant called Besse a Molletto and this deponent's Husband William Reynolds now deceased was a witness but whether the said Besse after the Expiration of her time from mr. Higginson was to be free from mr. Key this deponent cannot tell and mr. Higginson promised to use her as well if she were his own Child and further this deponent Saith not.

   Signum Ann Clark

   20th January 1655. Jurat in Curia

Elizabeth Newman aged 80 years or thereabouts Sworn and Examined Saith that she this deponent brought Elizabeth a Molletto, Servant to the Estate of Col. John Mottrom deceased to bed of two Children and she laid them both to William Grinsted and further this Deponent Saith not. Elizabeth Newman her mark 20th January 1655 Jurat in Curia

A Report of a Committee from an Assembly Concerning the freedom of Elizabeth Key

It appeareth to us that she is the daughter of Thomas Key by several Evidences and by a fine imposed upon the said Thomas for getting her mother with Child of the said Thomas That she hath been by verdict of a Jury impaneled 20th January 1655 in the County of Northumberland found to be free by several oaths which the Jury desired might be Recorded That by the Common Law the Child of a Woman slave begot by a freeman ought to be free That she hath been long since Christened Col. Higginson being her Godfather and that by report she is able to give a very good account of her faith That Thomas Key sold her only for nine years to Col. Higginson with several conditions to use her more Respectfully than a Common servant or slave That in case Col. Higginson had gone for England within nine years he was bound to carry her with him and pay her passage and not to dispose of her to any other For these Reasons we conceive the said Elizabeth ought to be free and that her last Master should give her Corn and Clothes and give her satisfaction for the time she hath served longer than She ought to have done. But forasmuch as no man appeared against the said Elizabeth's petition we think not fit a determinative Judgment should pass but that the County or Quarter Court where it shall be next tried to take notice of this to be the sense of the Burgesses of this present Assembly and that unless [original torn] shall appear to be executed and reasons [original torn] opposite part Judgment by the said Court be given accordingly.

   Charles Norwood Clerk Assembly

   James Gaylord hath deposed that this is a true copy James Gaylord

   21th July 1656 Jurat in Curia

   21th July 1656 This writing was recorded

At a Grand Assembly held at James City 20th of March 1655 Ordered that the whole business of Elizabeth Key [and?] the report of the Committee thereupon be returned to the County Court where the said Elizabeth Key liveth.

This is a true copy from the book of Records of the Order granted the last Assembly

   Teste Robert Booth

   21th July 1656 This Order of Assembly was Recorded

Upon the petition of George Colclough one of the overseers of Col. Mottrom his Estate that the cause concerning a Negro wench named Black Besse should be heard before the Governor and Councel Whereof in regard of the Order of the late Assembly referring the said case to the Governor and Councel at least upon Appeal made to them these are therefore in his Highness the Lord Protector his name to will and require the Commissioners of the County of Northumberland to Surcease from any further proceedings on the said Cause and to give notice to the parties interested therein to appear before the Governor at the next Quarter Court on the fourth day for a determination thereof. Given under my hand this 7th of June 1656.

   Edward Digges 21th 1656 This Writing was Recorded.

Whereas mr. George Colclough and mr. William Presly overseers of the Estate of Colonel John Mattrom deceased were Summoned to this Court at the suite of Elizabeth Key both Plaintiff and Defendant being present and no cause of action at present appearing The Court doth therefore order that the said Elizabeth Key shall be non-suited and that William Grinsted Attorney of the said Elizabeth shall by the tenth of November next pay fifty pounds of tobacco to the said overseers for a non-suite with Court charges else Execution. Whereas the whole business concerning Elizabeth Key by order of Assembly was Referred to this County Court. According to the Report of a Committee at an Assembly held at the same time which upon the Records of this County appears, It is the judgement of this Court that the Said Elizabeth Key ought to be free and forthwith to have Corn, Clothes, and Satisfaction according to the said Report of the Committee. Mr. William Thomas dissents from this judgment.

These are to Certify whom it may concern that William Greensted and Elizabeth Key intend to be joined in the Holy Estate of Matrimony. If anyone can show any Lawful cause why they may not be joined together let them Speak or ever after hold their tongues.

Signum William Greensted Signum Elizabeth Key 21th July 1656 this Certificate was Published in open Court and is Recorded

I Capt. Richard Wright administrator of the Estate of Col. John Mottrom deceased do assign and transfer unto William Grinstead a maid servant formerly belonging unto the Estate of the said Col. Mottrom commonly called Elizabeth Key being now Wife unto the said Grinstead and do warrant the said Elizabeth and do bind my Self to save her and the said Grinstead from any molestation or trouble that shall or futurely arise from or by any person or persons that shall pretend or claim any title or interest to any manor of service [original torn] from the said Elizabeth witness. my hand this 21th of July 1659

Test William Th[omas] Richard Wright
James Aust[en]

Land Patent Book (circa 1650s)

This brief excerpt reveals the way inheritances could pass from a father through his daughters to his sons-in-law, since daughters did not have legal standing on their own in colonial Virginia. Richard Thompson was the father of Sarah and Elizabeth; the former was married to Thomas Willoughby and the latter to Peter Presly. The two men effectively inherited the land through their marriages to Thompson's daughters.

Source: Warren M. Billings, ed., *The Old Dominion in the Seventeenth Century: A Documentary History of Virginia, 1660–1689*, rev. ed. (Chapel Hill: University of North Carolina Press for the Omohundro Institute of Early American History and Culture, 2007), 141.

The said Land being formerly granted unto Richard Tompson by two several Patents the one for Five hundred and Sixty Acres dated the fourth of april one thousand six hundred and fifty nine; the other for Forty eight Acres dated the fifteenth of December one thousand six hundred and fifty one, and after the [said] Richard Tompsons decease became due unto Sarah and Elizabeth Tompson Heirs of the aforesaid Richard and by Mr Thomas Willoughby and Mr Peter Presly who married the said Sarah and Elizabeth Tompson.

The Gloucester Conspiracy (1663)

The working and living conditions of servants and slaves was dire in midcentury Virginia, with high mortality rates. In 1657, the House of Burgesses recognized the difficulties of servants and the potential for uprising, passing a law allowing them to bring to court complaints of "harsh and bad usage, or else for want of diett or convenient necessaries." Nonetheless, uprising did occur.

On September 1, 1663, a handful of English servants met and conspired to gather arms and confront Governor Berkeley at Green Spring Plantation. Betrayed by Birkenhead, one of their own numbers, the servants were captured and tried; four were hanged. Birkenhead, however, was rewarded with his freedom and five thousand pounds of tobacco. The assembly also proclaimed an annual celebration of the defeat of this conspiracy.

Below are the extant records relating to the conspiracy. What do they reveal about the government's response to the conspiracy? What do they accuse the servants of and in what terms? What is revealed of the servants' concerns and their plans for the uprising?

What terms does the government use to describe Birkenhead's role in revealing the conspiracy?

If you were to consider joining a similar uprising, how does this event inform your thinking about necessary tactics, strategies, and the likelihood of success?

Source: Warren M. Billings, ed., *The Old Dominion in the Seventeenth Century: A Documentary History of Virginia, 1660–1689*, rev. ed. (Chapel Hill: University of North Carolina Press for the Omohundro Institute of Early American History and Culture, 2007), 167–72.

[A. Indictment of the Conspirators]
James City

The Jurors for our Sovereign Lord the King upon their oath present that John Gunter Late of the County of Gloucester Laborer Wm. Bell Late of the same Laborer, Richard Darbishire Late of the same Laborer, John Hayle Late of the same Laborer, Thomas Jones late of the same Laborer, Wm. Ball Late of the same Laborer, Wm. Poultney Late of the same Laborer, Wm. Bewdell Late of the same Laborer, and Thomas Collins Late of the same Laborer as false Traytors against his most Excellent Prince, our Sovereign Lord Charles the Second by the Grace of God King of England Scotland, France and Ireland and of his dominions thereunto Belonging Defender of the Faith and The fear of God in their hearts not having, nor weighing their due Allegiance but seduced by the Instigation of the devil, and intending wholy to wickedness, put out and Extinguish the hearty care and the love, and due Obedience which a true and faithful subject of the King should have, and by the Law is bound to bear towards our said Sovereign Lord The Sixth day of this instant September in the fifteenth year of the reign of our said Sovereign Lord the King at Newmans Land in the County of Glocester aforesaid Falsely, seditiously, and traitorously intended, imagined, went about, and Compassed the said King their Sovereign, and natural Liege Lord not only for his Royall State, title, Power, and government of this his Majesties Country of Virginia utterly to deprive depose, cast down, and disherit but to bring, and put the Right Honorable Sir Wm. Berkeley Knt his said Majesties Governor and Capt. Generall of this Country of Virginia from his Power Authority, and Government if he should oppose, or resist them in their wicked, and Rebellious proceedings, and also sedition in the said Country to raise up, and were to Levy and make and wholy to subvert and destroy the State of this Country of Virginia being in, and throughout well constituted, and ordered, and to the Intent they might fulfill, and bring to pass those their intents they the said John Gunter, Wm. Bell, Richard Darbishire, John Hayle, Thomas Jones, Wm. Ball, Wm. Poultney, Wm. Bewdell and Thomas Collings the day and year aforesaid at the place did Barberously meet together confer and treat concerning their traiterous purposes, immagination, compassings and Intents aforesaid, and by what means and manner they might be brought to pass and accomplished, and then and there they maliciously, and advisedly, and traiterously, did agree, design, intend, and determine the house of one Francis Willis in the County aforesaid Esquire one of the Councellors of State for this Country of Virginia to break and Enter, and all the Guns, Weapons, and other arms and ammunition of War there found, and seize upon and take away therewith to arme themselves, and Likewise house of one Katherine Cooke in the same county Widow in the Like manner to break and Enter and all Guns, Weapons and other Arms, and Ammunition of War to Seize upon and take away and therewith to arm certain other persons to the number of thirty, by them and with them through their false, malicious, and traterous procurments combyned and Engaged in the said trayterous, and rebellious purposes, imaginations, compassing, and Intents, and also to kill and Murder all and Every Person and Persons that should in any manner, or way resist, oppose, or hinder them in their wicked and rebellious proceedings, and sedition, to the utter Subversion of the state of this his Majesties Country and Contrary to the statutes in such Cases made to wit the 25 Ed. 3, [stat. 5] ca. 2 and 23 Eliz [English treason statutes] and against the peace of the Sovereign Lord the King his Crown and Dignties etc.

[B. Interrogation of the Conspirators]

The Examination of Thomas Collins of the County of Gloucester Laborer being Examined Saith

That upon the first day of this present September the said Collins went to acquaint [Bell?] that one Richard Darbishire about three days before did him the said Bell with the said Collins meet him and others at Mr. [Peter] Knights Little house in the wood about a design for their freedom where the said Collins and Bell did meet other Eight men, and there they did Continue, and agree that upon the Sunday night following about 12 of the Clock to meet at a place call the poplar spring, and to bring arms with them the said Collins intend to bring one of his Masters Col. [Thomas] Walkers [a Gloucester justice of the peace] Guns, and other ammunition, and from thence to march to the Right honorable the Governor and there to desire to be released of one year of their time which they had to serve, and their Capt. They would have Either Gunter, or Bell, and in case the Governor should deny to release them the said years service that then they would go forth of the Land if they Could to an Island which the said Collins doth not remember the name of, and saith not.

Thomas Collins
Taken by me the 13th of Sept. 1663
Robert Mitford his Majesties Attorney

The Examination of Willam Budell Taken the 8th of September before Lt. Col. Willis, mr. Abraham Iverson and Maj. John Smith who saith that being at a little house of mr. Peter Knights in the wood near unto mr. Cooks quarter where were present Eight servants, and my self, namely Wm. Bell, one Collins, Wm. Pultney, one Gunter Servant unto mr. [John] Pate, there we did move that an oath of Secrecy should pass for the concealment of our design which was as followeth, first that we all should meet at poplar spring on Sunday night next, and to bring with us what Company, arms, and ammunition we could get, and in the first place to go to the dwelling house of Lt. Col. Willis, and to seize on the arms and drum, and so to march to our freedom, and in Case that the Governor should refuse, to march out of the Country, and further that in case any there present should not condescend, and yield, and keep secret our intended design then we resolved to be the death of him, and further saith not.

Willam Budell

The Examination of William Bell then Examined doth aver and Confirm all the premisses aforesaid, and further saith that Richard Derbishire came unto me, and acquainted me of the aforesaid design above a month ago, and further saith not as witness my hand this 8th of September 1663.

The Examination of Thomas Collings taken the 8th of September 1663 saith that the persons abovementioned all resolv'd to meet next one Sunday night at poplar spring, and that the Company within mentioned did propose and offer unto Wm. Bell that the said Wm. Bell should be their Leader in the aforesaid design, but he would not accept of the offer, and

66 CORE TEXTS

further saith that he the said Collins was on Saturday night Last sent unto the said Bell by one Richard Derbishire that he the said Bell should come to Mrs. Cooks Quarter, and speak with the said Derbishire, and further saith not. Thomas Collins

The Examination of Wm. Poultney taken the 8th of September 1663 saith the he was present at a Little house of Mr. Knights on Saturday Last, and there were present the persons in the aforementioned Examination Specified, and there was agreed amongst them to make a Rising, and to march to Lt. Col. Willis his house, and to seize on his arms and Drum, and to Endeavour to Drumme their freedome, and further saith that Richard Darbishire first acquainted him the design, and further saith not.
The mark of
William W Poultney

The Examination of John Gunter taken the 9th of September 1663 who saith that on Last Sunday he was at a Little house in the woods where four more besides himself, but what they did hee will not Confess, only he saith that they were intended to go to the Governor about their freedom, and further saith not.
Jno. Gunter

The Examination of Thomas Jones taken the 9th of September 1663 who saith that on Sunday Last Jno. Gunter desired him to go to Maj. Smiths house, and desire Maj. Smiths Drummer to meet him at Jones his House, and so to go to mr. Knights Little house in the wood, and we three went, and met Six more nine in all whose names I Know not, and that on Sunday next we were to meet at Poplar spring, and there Gunter promised to bring what of Mr. Pates Servants he Could, and from poplar Spring we were resolved to march to Col. Willis house, and seize on his arms and ammunition, and drum, and so to march from house to house, and seize on what arms we could get and that Last Sunday was seventh day at night Gunter recalled to us, and then they shook hands, and [some surely?] to their Designs, and after all was done amongst us, then Bell, Gunter, and Derbishire had private Conferences amongst themselves, what it was I Know not, and further saith not as witness my hand.
Thomas Jones

The Examination of Wm. Ball, taken the 9th of September 1663, who saith that Jones told him Last Friday night that Sunday they were to meet at Mr. Knights house in the Woods, and desired me to go and Sunday I went with them, and there we met 9 in all, but what was their design I Know not, but only the Sunday night we were to meet at poplar spring, and further saith not.
the mark of
William X Ball

[It is not possible to follow this case further, owing to the destruction of the General Court records for this period.]

[C. The General Assembly Rewards John Berkenhead]

Whereas John Berkenhead Servant to Maj. John Smith of Glocester County did out of his honest affection to the preservation of this Country make discovery of a bloody design that some mutinous servants had contrived, which had it not been by Gods mercy thus unexpectedly prevented by a detection of the Principle Authors might have brought ruin and destruction to this his Majesties Country, The Assembly have Ordered That the said Berkenhead shall have his freedom given and five thousand pounds of tobo to be paid him this year in Gloster County out of the public Levie, as a reward to him for his good Service and an encouragement to others.

[D. The General Assembly Declares a Thanksgiving Day]

WHEREAS it is evident that certain mutinous villains had entered into such a desperate conspiracy as had brought an inevitable ruin to the country had not God in his infinite mercy prevented it, this grand assembly to testify their thanks to Almighty God for so miraculous a preservation have enacted that the thirteenth of September, the day this villainous plot should have been put into execution, be annually kept holy to keep the same in a perpetual commemoration.

George Alsop, *A Character of the Province of Mary-Land* (1666)

Social unrest in Virginia was tied also to the experience and condition of English servants. George Alsop was one of those servants, working in Maryland (neighbor of Virginia with a similar economy and social structure). Yet he took the position of promoter of the colonies. His tract, then, is a better example of seventeenth-century marketing than it is a reliable historical record of the servant experience. Nonetheless, one can appreciate the contrast between his positive description and the actual experience of servants (and slaves). Such a contrast between an idealized view and the lived experience of servants reflects the distance between the advantaged elite of the Chesapeake world and the masses at the bottom rungs of society.

What is Alsop's opinion of people's natural state of industriousness?

Based on his disclaimers, what kinds of concerns do servants have regarding their transportation to the colonies, nature of employment, conditions of service, and so forth?

What does he say concerning the availability of guns in the colony?

How long does an indenture typically last? What does the servant receive at the end of the term of service?

And what advantages do women have over men who come to the colonies as servants?

Source: George Alsop, *A Character of the Province of Mary-Land* (1966; repr., Baltimore, 1880), 53–60.

Chapter III. *The necessariness of Servitude proved, with the common usage of Servants in* Mary-Land, *together with their Privileges.*

There is no truer Emblem of Confusion either in Monarchy or Domestic Governments, than when either the Subject, or the Servant, strives for the upper hand of his Prince, or Master, and to be equal with him, from whom he receives his present subsistence: Why then, if Servitude be so necessary that no place can be governed in order, nor people live without it, this may serve to tell those which prick up their ears and bray against it, That they are none but Asses, and deserve the Bridle of a strict commanding power to rein them in: For I'm certainly confident, that there are several Thousands in most Kingdoms of Christendom, that could not at all live and subsist, unless they had served some prefixed time, to learn either some Trade, Art, or Science, and by either of them to extract their present livelihood.

Then methinks this may stop the mouths of those that will undiscreetly compassionate them that dwell under necessary Servitudes; for let but Parents of an indifferent capacity in Estates, when their Children's age by computation speak them seventeen or eighteen years old, turn them loose to the wide world, without a seven years working Apprenticeship (being just brought up to the bare formality of a little reading and writing) and you shall immediately see how weak and shiftless they'll be towards the maintaining and supporting of themselves; and (without either stealing or begging) their bodies like a Sentinel must continually wait to see when their Souls will be frighted away by the pale Ghost of a starving want.

Then let such, where Providence hath ordained to life as Servants, either in England or beyond Sea, endure the pre-fixed yoke of their limited time with patience, and then in a small computation of years, by an industrious endeavor, they may become Masters and Mistresses of Families themselves. And let this be spoke to the deserved praise of Mary-Land, That the four years I served there were not to me so slavish, as a two years Servitude of a Handicraft Apprenticeship was here in London. . . . Not that I write this to seduce or delude any, or to draw them from their native soil, but out of a love to my Countrymen, whom in the general I wish well to, and that the lowest of them may live in such a capacity of Estate, as that the bare interest of their Livelihoods might not altogether depend upon persons of the greatest extendments. . . .

They whose abilities cannot extend to purchase their own transportation over into Mary-Land, (and surely he that cannot command so small a sum for so great a matter, his life must needs be mighty low and dejected) I say they may for the debarment of a four years sordid liberty, go over into this Province and there live plenteously well. And what's a four years Servitude to advantage a man all the remainder of his days, making his predecessors happy in his sufficient abilities, which he attained to partly by the restrainment of so small a time?

Now those that commit themselves unto the care of the Merchant to carry them over, they need not trouble themselves with any inquisitive search touching their Voyage; for there is such an honest care and provision made for them all the time they remain aboard the Ship, and are sailing over, that they want for nothing that is necessary and convenient.

The Merchant commonly before they go aboard the Ship, or set themselves in any forwardness for their Voyage has Conditions of Agreements drawn between him and those that by a voluntary consent become his Servants, to serve him, his Heirs or Assigns, according as they in their primitive acquaintance have made their bargain, some two, some three, some four years; and whatever the Master or Servant ties himself up to here in England by Condition, the Laws of the Province will force a performance of when they come there: Yet here is this Privilege in it when they arrive, If they dwell not with the Merchant they made their first agreement withall, they may choose whom they will serve their prefixed time with; and after their curiosity has pitcht on one whom they think fit for their turn, and that they may live well withall, the Merchant makes an Assignment of the Indenture over to him whom they of their free will have chosen to be their Master, in the same nature as we here in England (and no otherwise) turn over Covenant Servants or Apprentices from one Master to another. Then let those whose chaps are always breathing forth those filthy dregs of abusive exclamations, . . . against this Country of Mary-Land, saying, That those which are transported over thither, are sold in open Market for Slaves, and draw in Carts like Horses; which is so damnable an untruth, that if they should search to the very Center of Hell, and enquire for a Lie of the most ancient and damned stamp, I confidently believe they could not find one to parallel this: For know, That the Servants here in Mary-Land of all Colonies, distant or remote Plantations, have the least cause to complain, either for strictness of Servitude, want of Provisions, or need of Apparel: Five days and a half in the Summer weeks is the allotted time that they work in; and for two months, when the Sun predominates in the highest pitch of his heat, they claim an ancient and customary Privilege, to repose themselves three hours in the day within the house, and this is undeniably granted to them that work in the Fields.

In the Winter time, which lasts three months (viz.) December, January, and February, they do little or no work or employment, save cutting of wood to make good fires to sit by, unless their Ingenuity will prompt them to hunt the Deer, or Bear, or recreate themselves in Fowling, to slaughter the Swans, Geese, and Turkeys (which this Country affords in a most plentiful manner:) For every Servant has a Gun, Powder and Shot allowed him, to sport him withall on all Holidays and leisurable times, if he be capable of using it, or be willing to learn. . . .

He that lives in the nature of a Servant in this Province, must serve but four years by the Custom of the Country; and when the expiration of his time speaks him a Freeman, there's a Law in the Province, that enjoins his Master whom he hath served to give him Fifty Acres of Land, Corn to serve him a whole year, three Suits of Apparel, with things necessary to them, and Tools to work withall; so that they are no sooner free, but they are ready to set up for themselves, and when once entered, they live passingly well.

The Women that go over into this Province as Servants, have the best luck here as in any place of the world besides; for they are no sooner on shore, but they are courted into a Copulative Matrimony, which some of them (for aught I know) had they not come to such a Market with their Virginity might have kept it by them until it had been moldy. . . . Men have not altogether so good luck as Women in this kind, or natural preferment, without they be good Rhetoricians, and well versed in the art of persuasion, then (probably) they may rivet themselves in the time of their Servitude into the private and reserved favor of their Mistress, if Age speak their Master deficient.

In short, touching the Servants of this Province, they live well in the time of their Service, and by their restraintment in that time, they are made capable of living much better when they come to be free; which in several other parts of the world I have observed, That after some servants have brought their indented and limited time to a just and legal period by Servitude, they have been much more incapable of supporting themselves from sinking into the Gulf of a slavish, poor, fettered, and entangled life, than all the fastness of their pre-fixed time did involve them in before.

Lower Norfolk County Court Minutes (1667)

As of 1667, the status of Afro-Virginians was not permanently established. Note several points in this petition for freedom by Fernando "a Negro": he claims the Christian faith (which the court suspects is a sham), he is a product of the Atlantic World, and the court refuses to investigate his statements, condemning him to slavery for life. Such cases demonstrated to Afro-Virginians how precarious was their place in Virginia society, yet they did not stop striving for freedom.

Source: Warren M. Billings, ed., *The Old Dominion in the Seventeenth Century: A Documentary History of Virginia, 1660–1689*, rev. ed. (Chapel Hill: University of North Carolina Press for the Omohundro Institute of Early American History and Culture, 2007), 200.

Whereas Fernando a Negro sued Capt. [John] Warner for his freedom pretending he was a Christian and had been several years in England and therefore ought to serve noe longer than any other servant that came out of England according to the custom of the Country and also Presented several papers in Portugal or some other language which the Court could not understand which he alleged were papers From several Governors where he had lived a freeman and where he was home. Wherefore the Court could find noe Cause wherefore he should be free but Judge him a slave for his life time, From which Judgement the said Negro hath appealed to the fifth day of the next Generall Court. [It is not possible to follow this case further owing to the destruction of the General Court records for this period.]

Sir William Berkeley, "Enquiries to the Governor of Virginia from the Lords Commissioners of Foreign Plantations" (1671)

The "lords commissioners of foreign plantations" sent a set of questions to the governor of Virginia, Sir William Berkeley, in 1670. He returned his answers to England the following year, and they reveal many aspects of the colony but also expose Berkeley's distinct perspective on it.

What is the status of the military in the colony?

How does the governor describe relations with the Native Americans of Virginia?

To what degree is Virginia's economy diversified beyond the production of tobacco?

How many people live in the colony? What is their status? What racial distinctions does the governor make? Are Native Americans included in the account?

What taxes are paid in the colony?

What can you observe of the governor's perspectives on religion and education?

Source: William Waller Hening, ed., *The Statutes at Large; Being a Collection of the Laws of Virginia, From the First Session of the Legislature, in the Year 1619* (New York: R&W&G Bartow, 1823), 2:511–17.

1. What councils, assemblies, and courts of judicature are within your government, and of what nature and kind?

    Answer. There is a governor and sixteen counselors, who have from his sacred majesty, a commission of *Oyer and Terminer*, who judge and determine all causes that are above fifteen-pound sterling; for what is under, there are particular courts in every county, which are twenty in number. Every year, at least the assembly is called, before whom lie appeals, and this assembly is composed of two Burgesses out of every county. These lay the necessary taxes, as the necessity of the war with the Indians, or their exigencies require.

2. What courts of judicature are within your government relating to the admiralty?

    Answer. In twenty-eight years there has never been one prize brought into the country; so that there is no need for a particular court for that concern.

3. Where are the legislative and executive powers of your government seated?

    Answer. In the governor, council and assembly, and officers substituted by them.

4. What statute laws and ordinances are now made and in force?

    Answer. The secretary of this country every year sends to the lord chancellor, or one of the principal secretaries, what laws are yearly made; which for the most part concern our own private exigencies; for, contrary to the laws of England, we never did, nor dare make any, only this, that no sale of land is good and legal, unless within three months after the conveyance it be recorded in the general court, or county courts.

5. What number of horse and foot are within your government, and whether they be trained bands or standing forces?

    Answer. All our freemen are bound to be trained every month in their particular counties, which we suppose, and do not much mistake in the calculation, are near eight thousand horse: there are more, but it is too chargeable for poor people, as we are, to exercise them.

6. What castles and forts are within your government, and how situated, as also what stores and provision they are furnished withal?

    Answer. There are five forts in the country, two in James river and one in the three other rivers of York, Rappahannock, and Potomac; but God knows we have neither skill or ability to make or maintain them; for there is not, nor, as far as my inquiry can reach, ever was one engineer in the country, so that we are at continual charge to repair unskillful and inartificial building of that nature. There is not above thirty great and serviceable guns; this we yearly supply with powder and shot as far as our utmost abilities will permit us.

7. What number of privateers do frequent your coasts and neighboring seas; what their burthens are; the number of their men and guns, and the names of their commanders?

    Answer. None to our knowledge, since the late Dutch war.

8. What is the strength of your bordering neighbors, be they Indians or others, by sea and land; what correspondence do you keep with your neighbors?

    Answer. We have no Europeans seated nearer to us than St. Christophers or Mexico that we know of, except some few French that are beyond New England. The Indians, our neighbors are absolutely subjected, so that there is no fear of them. As for correspondence, we have none with any European strangers; nor is there a possibility to have it with our own nation further than our traffic concerns.

9. What arms, ammunition and stores did you find upon the place, or have been sent you since, upon his majesty's account; when received; how employed; what quantity of them is there remaining, and where?

    Answer. When I came into the country, I found one only ruinated fort, with eight great guns, most unserviceable, and all dismounted but four, situated in a most unhealthy place, and where, if an enemy knew the soundings, he could keep out of the danger of the best guns in Europe. His majesty, in the time of the Dutch war, sent us thirty great guns, most of which were lost in the ship that brought them. Before, or since this, we never had one great or small gun sent us, since my coming hither; nor, I believe, in twenty years before. All that have been sent by his sacred majesty, are still in the country, with a few more we lately bought.

10. What monies have been paid or appointed to be paid by his majesty, or levied within your government for and toward the buying of arms or making or maintaining of any fortifications or castles, and how have the said monies been expended?

    Answer. Besides those guns I mentioned, we never had any monies of his majesty towards the buying of ammunition or building of forts. What monies can be spared out of the public revenue, we yearly lay out in ammunition.

11. What are the boundaries and contents of the land, within your government?

    Answer. As for the boundaries of our land, it was once great, ten degrees in latitude, but now it has pleased his majesty to confine us to half a degree. Knowingly, I speak this. Pray God it may be for his majesty's service, but I much fear the contrary.

12. What commodities are there of the production, growth and manufacture of your plantation; and particularly, what materials are there already growing, or may be produced for shipping in the same?

    Answer. Commodities of the growth of our country, we never had any but tobacco, which in this yet is considerable, that it yields his majesty a great revenue; but of late, we have begun to make silk, and so many mulberry trees are planted, and planting, that if we had skillful men from Naples or Sicily to teach us the art of making it perfectly, in less than half an age, we should make as much silk in a year as England did yearly expend three score years since; but now we hear it is grown to a greater excess, and more common and vulgar usage. Now, for shipping, we have admirable masts and very good oaks; but for iron ore I dare not say there is sufficient to keep one iron mill going for seven years.

13. Whether salt-petre is or may be produced within your plantation, and if so, at what rate may it be delivered in England?

    Answer. Salt-petre, we know of none in the country.

14. What rivers, harbors or roads are there in or about your plantation and government, and of what depth and soundings are they?

    Answer. Rivers, we have four, as I named before, all able, safely and severally to bear and harbor a thousand ships of the greatest burden.

15. What number of planters, servants, and slaves; and how many parishes are there in your plantation?

    Answer. We suppose, and I am very sure we do not much miscount, that there is in Virginia above forty thousand persons, men, women, and children, and of which there are two thousand black slaves, six thousand Christian servants, for a short time, the rest are born in the country or have come in to settle and seat, in bettering their condition in a growing country.

16. What number of English, Scots, or Irish have for these seven years last past come yearly to plant and inhabit within your government; as also what blacks or slaves have been brought in within the said time?

    Answer. Yearly, we suppose there comes in, of servants, about fifteen hundred, of which most are English, few Scotch, and fewer Irish, and not above two or three ships of negroes in seven years.

17. What number of people have yearly died, within your plantation and government for these seven years last past, both whites and blacks?

    Answer. All new plantations are, for an age or two, unhealthy, till they are thoroughly cleared of wood; but unless we had a particular register office, for the denoting of all that died, I cannot give a particular answer to this query, only this I can say, that there is not often unseasoned hands (as we term them) that die now, whereas heretofore not one of five escaped the first year.

18. What number of ships do trade yearly to and from your plantation, and of what burden are they?

    Answer. English ships, near eighty come out of England and Ireland every year for tobacco; few New England ketches; but of our own, we never yet had more than two at one time, and those not more than twenty tons burden.

19. What obstructions do you find to the improvement of the trade and navigation of the plantations within your government?

    Answer. Mighty and destructive, by that severe act of parliament which excludes us the having any commerce with any nation in Europe but our own, so that we cannot add to our plantation any commodity that grows out of it, as olive trees, cotton, or vines. Besides this, we cannot procure any skillful men for one now hopeful commodity, silk; for it is not lawful for us to carry a pipe stave, or a barrel of corn, to any place in Europe out of the king's dominions. If this were for his majesty's service or the good of his subjects, we should not repine, whatever our sufferings are for it; but on my soul, it is contrary for both. And this is the cause why no small or great vessel are built here; for we are most obedient to all laws, whilst the New England men break through, and men trade to any place that their interest leads them.

20. What advantages or improvements do you observe that may be gained to your trade and navigation.

    Answer. None, unless we had liberty to transport our pipe staves, timber, and corn to other places besides the king's dominions.

21. What rates and duties are charged and payable upon any goods exported out of your plantation, whither of your own growth or manufacture, or otherwise, as also upon goods imported?

    Answer. No goods either exported or imported, pay any the least duties here, only two shillings the hogshead on tobacco exported, which is to defray all public charges; and this year we could not get an account of more than fifteen thousand hogsheads, out of which the king allows me a thousand *[pounds sterling]* yearly, with which I must maintain the port of my place, and one hundred intervening charges that cannot be put to public account. And I can knowingly affirm, that there is no government of ten years settlement, but has thrice as much allowed him. But I am supported by my hopes, that his gracious majesty will one day consider me.

22. What revenues do or may arise to his majesty within your government, and of what nature is it; by whom is the same collected, and how answered and accounted to his majesty?

    Answer. There is no revenue arising to his majesty but out of the quit-rents; and this he has given away to a deserving servant, Col. Henry Norwood.

23. What course is taken about instructing the people, within your government in the Christian religion; and what provision is there made for the paying of your ministry?

    Answer. The same course that is taken in England out of towns; every man according to his ability instructing his children. We have forty-eight parishes, and our ministers are well paid, and by my consent should be better if they would pray oftener and preach less. But of all other commodities, so of this the worst are sent us, and we had few that we could boast of, since the persecution in Cromwell's tyranny drove divers worthy men hither. But, I thank God, there are no free schools nor printing, and I hope we shall not have these hundred years; for learning has brought disobedience, and heresy, and sects into the world, and printing has divulged them, and libels against the best government. God keep us from both!

Francis Payne, "A Free Negro Property Owner in Colonial Virginia Bequeaths His Property" (1673)

Although race-based slavery was practiced from the moment the first Africans arrived in Virginia, it was also true that in some rare circumstances, individual Africans and those of African descent were able to escape the bonds of permanent servitude in the mid-seventeenth century. Francis Payne, a character in this game, was one of these.

Consider the advantages he had as a free person of color and the assumptions he made based on his status. What evidence can be found here that proves his assumptions were warranted? In what ways had Payne become acculturated to Anglo-Virginian society?

Source: Warren M. Billings, ed., *The Old Dominion in the Seventeenth Century: A Documentary History of Virginia, 1660–1689*, rev. ed. (Chapel Hill: University of North Carolina Press for the Omohundro Institute of Early American History and Culture, 2007), 181–82.

In the Name of god Amen I Francis Payne of Northampton County in Virginia being sick of body but of perfect knowledge and understanding and being willing to ease my mind of all worldly care Do make this my last will and Testament as follows

Imprimis I bequeath my soul to my loving Father my creator and to Jesus Christ who by his blood and passion suffered for my sins and all the world trustinge through his merit to enjoy that heavenly portion prepared for me and all true believers And as for my body I bequeath it unto the ground from whence it came there to receive a Christian burial And as for my worldly Estate I do give and bequeath it unto my loving wife Agnes *[Amy]* Payne my whole Estate real and personal moveables and immoveables making her my Indubitable Executrix of this my last will and Testament. And Do here declare that by virtue of these presents all former wills by me made and signed are rebuked and made void and this is to be my last will and Testament. And desire that my debts may in the first place be paid. In Testimony whereof I have subscribed my hand and put my seal this 9th day of May Anno Domini 1673.

Unto each of our god children a Cow Calf a piece when they attain to lawful age. but as for [Deura?] Driggins he is to have nothing by this will

Francis X Payne
his marke
Signed sealed and delivered in the presence of us
Nathaniel Wilkins
the marke of
Elizabeth X Pettit

The 29th day of September 1673. This day the last will and Testament of Francis Payne Negro was proved in open Court by the Corporal oath of Nathaniel Wilkins and allowed of and ordered to be Recorded (Provided that Elizabeth Pettitt the other evidence appear at the next Court and Confirm the probate thereof if living and of ability to own then or otherwise as sure as she can)

Test Daniel Neech Deputy Clerk
Recorded the 4th of October 1673. Daniel Neech Deputy Clerk

Council Minutes (1674)

The following selected council minutes offer a window into the political affairs of the colony and the ways that personal relationships intersected with them. Note, for example, the extreme degree to which the council goes to protect the dignity of its members and the extremity of the penalties levied. Notice, too, how often penalties are directly tied to the economy of the colony. Finally, observe the role the council plays in adjudicating matters of personal property and probates (handling of an individual's property after the person's passing) and the nonchalant way in which enslaved Afro-Virginian laborers are included in such business.

Source: Warren M. Billings, ed., *The Old Dominion in the Seventeenth Century: A Documentary History of Virginia, 1660–1689*, rev. ed. (Chapel Hill: University of North Carolina Press for the Omohundro Institute of Early American History and Culture, 2007), 69–71.

The Ninth Aprill 1674
present
GOVERNOR [Sir William Berkeley]
Edward Diggs
Col. [Nathaniel] Bacon
Col. [Thomas] Swann
Henry Corbyn
Col. [Thomas] Beale
Lt. Col. [Daniel] Parke
Thomas Ballard
Col. [Joseph] Bridger
Esquires

Whereas it Appears to this Court that Marmaduke Newton Did most wickedly and maliciously abuse Col. Nathaniel Bacon [*Nathaniel Bacon, the elder, uncle to Nathaniel Bacon, after whom the later rebellion is named*] one of his majesties Councell of State in most abusive Language this Court have thought fitt that the Said Newton be fined Twenty pound sterling but upon his Submission in Court It is ordered he pay two barrels of powder one to James City fort and the other to Nanzemond fort, And Ask the Said Col. Bacon forgiveness upon his Knees (which he Accordingly Did) and pay all Costs Lt. Col. William Cole and Major [Miles] Carey are Empowered to receive the powder and to be Accountable to both forts. . . .

It is ordered Mr. Richard Laurence be fined four hundred pound tobacco and Caske which is to Go towards the fort at James City, for Entertaining the Honorable Governors Servants.

Whereas It Appears to this Court that Peter Starke hath A better right to The Land that Anthony Vauson Escheated [*land that had reverted to the crown because there were no heirs*] in Yorke County, It is therefore ordered that the Said vauson Assign over all his rights of the Said Escheate to the Said Starkey, and that Starkey pay unto the Said Vauson fifteen hundred pound of tobacco and Caske in full [payment] of all charges Suspended by him in and about the Escheate. . . .

Whereas Mr. Samuel Arnall Did in his life time Convey to Lt. Col. [John] West a Certain Plantation with the Appurtenances in New Kent County for Ten Thousand pound of Tobacco and Caske and one John Wilson who married the Relict [widow] of the Said Arnall being in possession of the Same and pretending that the Said Land was made over only in Trust to the Said Lt. Col. John West and the matter being fully heard by this Court It is the Opinion of this Court that the Conveyance is Good, It is therefore ordered that the Sherriffe of New Kent Doe forthwith putt the Said Lt. Col. John West in possession of the Said Land but that upon payment to Lt. Col. John [West] of the Said Ten Thousand pound of tobacco and Caske the Same Shall return and be Rendered by the Said Lt. Col. West to Such persons of whom of right it belongs, And the Said Lt. Col. John West hath Judgment Against the personal Estate of the Said Arnall In the hands of the [said] Wilson for payment of Two Thousand one hundred Sixty Six pound of tobacco and Caske Nine hundred pound of Muscavado Sugar and one able man Negro with Costs.

Upon the Petition of Captain John West on behalf of himself and the rest of the Administrators of Col. Edmund Scarburgh Deceased Concerning A negro woman called black mary purchased by the Said Administrators from Col. John Vassall, It is ordered that the Said negroe woman return to her Service, And that the Administrators Aforesaid with the first opportunity take Care to write to Col. Vassall to know whether the Said negroe woman was A Slave or free, and if Appear she was no slave when bought, then they to pay her for her Service what this Court shall Adjudge.

Thomas Mathew, "The Beginning, Progress, and Conclusion of Bacon's Rebellion, 1675–1676" (1705)

Thomas Mathew, a planter and character in this game, wrote a narrative of Bacon's Rebellion thirty years after the fact in response to a request by Robert Harley, Lord Oxford, Minister of State to Queen Anne. Yet in the absence of contemporary accounts, and because Mathew not only was an eyewitness but was also involved in the initial violent encounters with the Doeg Indians, an excerpt of his narrative—the portion describing the initial violent encounters with the Native people in 1675—is included at this point in the chronology. Although he acknowledged at the time of writing that "divers occurrances are laps'd out of mind, and others imperfectly retained," Mathew's account may be treated in the game as a firsthand account from the time of the events described.

What hostilities were committed? Who were the perpetrators? The victims?

Source: Charles M. Andrews, ed., *Narratives of the Insurrections, 1675–1690* (New York: Charles Scribner's Sons, 1915), 16–17.

My Dwelling was in Northumberland, the lowest County on Potomack River, Stafford being the upmost; where having also a Plantation, Servants, Cattle, etc. My Overseer there had agreed with one Robt. Hen to come thither, and be my Herdsman, who then Lived Ten Miles above it; But on a Sabbath day Morning in the summer Anno 1675, People on their Way to Church, Saw this Hen lying th'wart his Threshold, and an Indian without the Door, both Chopped on their Heads, Arms and other Parts, as if done with Indian Hatchetts. The Indian was dead, but Hen when ask'd who did that? Answered "Doegs Doegs," and soon Died, then a Boy came out from under a Bed, where he had hid himself, and told them, Indians had come at break of day and done those Murders.

From this Englishman's blood did (by Degrees) arise Bacon's Rebellion with the following Mischiefs which Over-spread all Virginia and twice endangered Maryland, as by the ensuing Account is Evident.

Of this horrid Action Coll: Mason who commanded the Militia Regiment of Foot and Capt. Brent the Troop of Horse in that County, (both dwelling Six or Eight Miles Downwards) having speedy notice raised 30 or more men, and pursu'd those Indians 20 Miles up and 4 Miles over that River into Maryland, where landing at Dawn of Day, they found two small Paths. Each Leader with his Party took a Separate Path and in less than a furlong, either found a Cabin, which they Silently Surrounded. Capt. Brent went to the Doeg's Cabin (as it proved to be) Who Speaking the Indian Tongue Called to have a Matchacomicha Weewhip i.e. a Council, called presently Such being the usual manner with Indians. The King came Trembling forth, and would have fled, when Capt. Brent, Catching hold of his twisted lock (which was all the Hair he wore) told him he was come for the Murderer of *[Virginians on the Mathew plantation]*, the King pleaded ignorance and slipped loose, whom Brent shot dead with his pistol. The Indians shot two or three guns out at the door and fled, the English shot as many as they could, so that they killed ten, as Capt. Brent told me, and brought away the king's son of about 8 years old, concerning whom is an observable passage, at the end of this expedition; the noise of this shooting awakened the Indians in the Cabin which Col. Mason had Encompassed, who likewise rushed out and fled, of whom his Company (supposing from what Noise of Shooting Brent's party to be Engaged) shot (as the Col. informed me) Fourteen before *[a friendly]* Indian Came, who with both hands shook him (friendly) by an arm Saying *Susquehanougs Netoughs* i.e. Susquehanaugh friends, and fled, Whereupon *[the colonel]* ran amongst his Men, Crying out, "For the Lord's sake shoot no more, these are our friends the Susquehannocks."

John Easton, "A Relation of the Indian War" (1675)

In New England, the collection of English colonies in North America that lay northeast of the Chesapeake, war broke out between the native Algonquian people and the English settlers during the winter of 1674-75, six months before the violence on Thomas Mathew's farm. Named for Metacom, leader of the Wampanoags who was known by the English as King Philip, it was the deadliest war in American history up to this point. In seventeenth-century America, distances were farther than they are today and news traveled slowly, but rumors of conflict reached Virginia by late August. To simulate the availability of that news to Virginians, the following account is included. It was drafted by Quaker pacifist John Easton, attorney general of the Rhode Island colony, and bears his particular outlook. He was not simply an observer, but an active participant, having served as a mediator between the two sides and meeting with Metacom in June 1675. The negotiations failed to stem the tide of violence; the New Englanders launched a major offensive later in the summer. The account continues to the end of 1675.

Source: Franklin B. Hough, ed., *A Narrative of the Causes Which Led to Philip's Indian War* (Albany, NY: J. Munsell, 1858), 1-31.

True relation of what I know and of reports, and my understanding concerning the beginning and progress of the war now between the English and the Indians.

In the winter in the year 1674, an Indian was found dead, and by a Coroner's inquest of Plymouth Colony judged murdered. He was found dead in a hole through ice broken in a pond, with his gun and some fowl by him. Some English supposed him thrown in. Some Indians that I judged intelligible and impartial in that case did think he fell in, and was so drowned and that the ice did hurt his throat, as the English said it was cut; but they acknowledged that sometimes naughty Indians would kill others but not, as ever they heard, to obscure it, as if the dead Indian was not murdered. The dead Indian was called Sausimun and was a Christian that could read and write. Report was that he was a bad man; and that King Philip got him to write his will and that he made the writing for a great part of the land to be his, but read it as if it had been as Philip would have it; but it came to be known, and then he ran away from him.

Now one Indian informed that three Indians had murdered him, and showed a coat that he said they gave him to conceal them; the Indians report that the informer had played away his coat, and these men sent him that coat, and afterwards demanded pay, and he, so as not to pay, accused them, and knowing it would please the English so, to think him a better Christian. And the report came, that the three Indians had confessed and accused Philip so to employ them, and that the English would hang Philip, so the Indians were afraid, and reported that the English had flattered them (or by threats) to belie Philip that they might kill him to have his Land; and that if Philip had done it, it was their Law so to execute whomever their kings judged deserved it, and that he had no cause to hide it.

So Philip kept his Men in Arms. Plymouth Governor required him to disband his men and informed him his Jealousy was false. Philip answered he would do no harm and thanked the Governor for his Information.

The three Indians were hanged, to the last denied the Fact; but one broke the Halter as it is reported, then desired to be saved, and so was a little while, then confessed they three had done the Fact; and then he was hanged. And it was reported Sausimun before his death had informed of the Indian Plot, and that if the Indians knew it they would kill him, and that the Heathen might destroy the English for their Wickedness, as God had permitted the Heathen to destroy the Israelites of old. So the English were afraid and Philip was afraid, and both increased in Arms. But for forty years' time, Reports and jealousies of War had been very frequent, that we did not think that now a War was breaking forth; but about a Week before it did, we had Cause to think it would. Then to endeavor to prevent it, we lent a Man to Philip, that is he would come to the Ferry we would come over to speak with him. About four Miles we had to come; thither our Messenger come to them; they not aware of it behaved themselves as furious, but suddenly appeased when they understood who he was and what he came for, he called his Counsel and agreed to come to us; came himself unarmed, and about 40 of his Men armed. Then 5 of us went over, 3 were Magistrates. We sat very friendly together. We told him our business was to endeavor that they might not receive or do wrong. They said that was well; they had done no wrong, the English wronged them. We said we knew the English said the Indians wronged them, and the Indians said the English wronged them, but our Desire was the Quarrel might rightly be decided, in the best Way, and not as Dogs decided their Quarrels. The Indians owned that fighting was the worst Way; then they propounded how Right might take Place. We said, by Arbitration. They said that all English agreed against them, and so by Arbitration they had had much wrong; many Miles square of Land so taken from them, for English would have English Arbitrators; and once they were persuaded to give in their Arms, that thereby Jealousy might be removed, and the English having their Arms would not deliver them as they had promised, until they consented to pay a *100po*, (100 pounds) and now they had not so much Sum or Money; that they were as good be killed as leave all their Livelihood.

We said they might choose an Indian King and the English might choose the Governor of New York, that neither had Case to say either were Parties in the Difference. They said they had not heard of that Way, and said we honestly spoke, so we were persuaded if that Way had been tendered they would have accepted. We did endeavor not to hear their Complaints, said it was not convenient for us now to consider of, but to endeavor to prevent War; we said to them when in War against English, Blood was spilt, that engaged all Englishmen, for we were to be all under one King; we knew what their Complaints would be, and in our Colony had removed some of them in sending for Indian Rulers insofar as the Crime concerned Indians' Lives, which they very lovingly accepted, and agreed with us to their Execution, and said so they were able to satisfy their Subjects when they knew an Indian suffered duly, but said in what was only between their Indians and not in Townships, that we had purchased, they would not have us prosecute, and that they had a great Fear to have any of their Indians should be called or forced to be Christian Indians. They said that such were in everything more mischievous; only Dissemblers, and then the English made them not subject to their own Kings, and by their lying to wrong their Kings. We knew it to be true, and we promising them that however in Government to Indians all should be alike, and that we knew it was our King's will it should be so, that although we were weaker than other Colonies, they having submitted to our King to protect them, Others dared, not otherwise to molest them; so they expressed they took that to be well, that we had little Case to doubt, but that to us under the King they would have yielded to our Determinations in what any should have complained to us against them.

But Philip charged it to be dishonesty in us to put off the Hearing of the just Complaints, therefore we consented to hear them. They said they had been the first in doing Good to the English, and the English the first in doing wrong; said when the English first came, their King's Father was as a great Man, and the English as a little Child; he constrained other Indians from wronging the English, and gave them Corn and showed them how to plant, and was free to do them any Good, and had let them have a 100 Times more Land than now the King had for his own People. But their King's Brother, *[Massasoit]* when he was King, came miserably to die by being forced to Court, as they judged poisoned. And another Grievance was, if 20 of their honest Indians testified that a Englishman had done them wrong, it was as nothing; and if but one of their worst Indians testified against any Indian or their King, when it pleased the English it was sufficient. Another Grievance was, when their King sold Land, the English would say, it was more than they agreed to, and a Writing must be proven against all them, and some of their Kings had done wrong to sell so much. He left his people none, and some being given to Drunkenness the English made them drunk and then cheated them in Bargains, but now their Kings were forewarned not to part with Land, for nothing in Comparison to the Value thereof. Now home the English had owned for King or Queen, they would disinherit, and make another King that would give or sell them these Lands; that now, they had no Hopes left to keep any Land. Another Grievance, the English Cattle and Horses still increased; that when they removed 30 Miles from where English had anything to do, they could not keep their Corn from being spoiled, they never being used to fence, and thought when the English bought Land of them they would have kept their Cattle upon their own Land. Another Grievance, the English were so eager to sell the Indians Lickers, that most of the Indians spent all in Drunkenness, and then ravened upon the sober Indians, and they did believe often did hurt the English Cattle, and their King could not prevent it.

We knew before, these were their grand Complaints, but then we only endeavored to persuade that all Complaints might be righted without War but could have no other Answer but that they had not heard of that Way for the Governor of York and an Indian King to have the Hearing of it. We had Cause to think that had it been tendered it would have been accepted. We endeavored that however they Should lay down the War, for the English were too strong for them; they said, then the English should do to them as they did when they were too strong for the English.

So we departed without any discourteousness, and suddenly had a letter from Plymouth's Governor saying that they intended in arms to conform Philip, but giving no information what it was that they required or what terms he refused to have their quarrel decided, and in a week's time after we had been with the Indians the war was thus begun. . . .

When winter was come we had a letter from Boston of the United Commissioners that they were resolved to reduce the Narragansetts to conformity, so as not to be troubled with them anymore, and desired some help of boats and otherwise if we saw cause, and that we should keep secret concerning it. Our governor sent them word that we were satisfied the Narragansetts were treacherous and had aided Philip, and as we had assisted to relieve their army before, so we should be ready to assist them still, and advised that terms might be tendered that such might expect compensation that would not accept to engage in war and that there might be a separation between the guilty and the innocent, which in war could not be expected, we were not in the least expecting that they would have begun the war and not before proclaimed it or not give them defiance.

I having often informed the Indians that English men would not begin a war otherwise, it was brutish so to do. I am sorry that the Indians have cause to think me deceitful, for the English thus began the war with the Narragansetts after we had sent off our Island many Indians and informed them, if they kept by the watersides and did not meddle, that the English would do them no harm; although it was also not safe for us to let them live here. The army first took all those prisoners, then fell upon the Indian houses, burned them, and killed some men. The war began without proclamation; and some of our people did not know the English had begun mischief to the Indians, and being confident and having cause to be so, believed that the Indians would not hurt them before the English began. So they did not keep their garrison exactly. But the Indians, having received that mischief, came unexpectedly upon them and destroyed 145 of them beside other great loss. But the English army commanders say that they supposed Connecticut forces would have been there. They sold the Indians that they had taken as aforesaid, for slaves, except for one old man that was carried off our Island upon his son's back. He was so decrepit that War was declared by the Commissioners at Boston on September 9, 1675. In October the size of the war force was increased and Josiah Winslow of

Plymouth placed in command. He could not go, and when the army took them, his son upon his back carried him to the garrison. Some would have had him devoured by dogs, but the tenderness of some of them prevailed to cut off his head. And afterwards they came suddenly upon the Indians where the Indians had prepared to defend themselves, and so received and did much mischief. And for about six weeks since, the time has been spent by both parties to recruit; and now the English army is out to seek after the Indians, but it is most likely that those most able to do mischief will escape, and the women and children and impotent may be destroyed; and so the most able will have the less encumbrance to doing mischief.

But I am confident it would be best for English and Indians that a peace were made upon honest terms for each to have a due propriety and to enjoy it without oppression or usurpation by one to the other. But the English dare not trust the Indians' promises; neither the Indians to the English's promises; and each has great cause therefore. I see no way likely unless a cessation from arms might be procured until it might be known what terms King Charles would propound, for we have great cause to think the Narragansett kings would trust our king and that they would have accepted him to be umpire if it had been tendered about any difference, for we do know the English have had much contention against those Indians to invalidate the kings determination for Narragansett to be in our colony, and we have cause to think it was the greatest cause of the war against them.

I see no means likely to procure a cessation from arms unless the Governor of New York can find a way to intercede; and so it will be likely a peace may be made without troubling our king. It has always been a principle in our Colony that there should be but one supreme authority for Englishmen both in our native country and wherever English have jurisdiction; and so we know that no English should begin a war and not first offer for the king to be umpire, and not persecute those that will not conform to their worship, even if their worship be what is not owned by the king. The king would not mind to have such things redressed; some may take it that he has not the power, and that there may be a way for them to take power in opposition to him. I am persuaded that New England's priests are so blinded by the spirit of persecution and anxious to have their hire and to have more room to be mere hirelings, that they have been the cause that the law of nations and the law of arms have been violated in this war, and that the war would not have been started if there had not been a hireling who, for his management of what he calls the gospel, to have it spread by violence, and to have his gain from his quarters paid for; and if any magistrates are unwilling to act as their pack horses, they will be trumpeting for innovation or war.

5th of 12th month 1675, Rhode Island.

JOHN EASTON

"The History of Bacon's and Ingram's Rebellion in Virginia, and in 1676"

Although the author of this account is unknown and the document was unknown until the eighteenth century, it appears to be a firsthand account written shortly after the time of the rebellion by someone familiar with the events. The author was clearly not a supporter of Bacon or of the governor. Given the limited records available at the time, we have elected to include a portion of this account that relates to affairs in the year before March 1676.

In what ways does the author criticize Bacon?
How is the narrative critical of Berkeley?

Source: Charles Deane, ed., *The History of Bacon's and Ingram's Rebellion in Virginia, and in 1676* (Cambridge, MA: J. Wilson and Son, 1867).

They found that their store was too short to endure a long Siege, without making empty bellies and that empty bellies, makes weak hearts, which always makes an unfit Serving Man to wait upon the God of war. Therefore they were resalue, before that their spirits were down, to do what they could to keep their stores up; as opportunity should befriend them. And although they were by the Law of Arms (as the case now stood) prohibited the hunting of wild Deer, they resalued to see what good might be done by hunting tame Horses. Which trade became their sport so long that those who came on Horseback to the siege, began to fear they should be compelled to trot home afoot, and glad if they scap'd so too: for these beleaguered blades made so many salleys, and the besiegers kept such negligent guards, that there was very few days passed without some remarkable mischief. But what can hold out all ways? euen stone walls yields to the not to be gain-said summons of time. And all though it is said that the Indians doth the least mind their Bellies (as being content with a little) of any people in the world, yet now their bellies began to mind them, and there stomachs too, which began to be more inclineable to peace, then war; which was the cause (no more Horse flesh being to be had) that they sent out 6 of their Worawances (chief men) to commence a treaty. What the Articles were, that they brought along with them, to treat of, I do not know; but certainly they were so unacceptable to the English, that they caused the Commissioners brains to be knock'd out, for dictating so badly to their tongues; which yet, 'tis possible, expressed more reason than the English had, to prove the lawfulness of this action, being Diametrical to the Law of Arms.

This strange action put those in the Fort to their trumps, having thus lost some of their prime court cards, without a fair dealing. They could not well tell what interpretation to put upon it (nor indeed, nobody else) and very faine they wo[uld] . . . why those, whom they sent out with a [view] to suplicate a peace should be worse dealt with than [those who] were sent out with a sword to denounce a war; but, [no one] could be got to make inquiry into the reason of this . . . which put them upon a resolution to forsake their [station, and] not to expostulate the cause any further. Having [made] this resolution and destroyed all things in the fort, that might be servisable to the English, they boldly, undiscovered, slip through the Leaguer (leaving the English to prosecute the siege, as Schogin's wife brooded the eggs that the Fox had suck'd) in the passing of which they knocked ten men over the head, who lay carelessly asleep in their way. Now although it might be said that the Indians went their ways empty handed, in regard they had left all their plunder and wealth behind them in the fort, yet it cannot be thought that they went away empty hearted: For though that was pretty well drained from it's former courage, through those inconveniencies that they had been subjected to, by the siege, yet in ye room thereof, rather than the venticles should lie void, they had stowed up so much mallize, intermixed with a resolution of revenge, for the affront that the English had put upon them, in killing their messengers of peace, that they resalued to commence a most barbarous and most bloody war.

The Besiegers having spent a great deal of ill employed time in pecking at the husk, and now finding the shell open, and missing the expected prey, did not a little wonder what was become of the lately impounded Indians, who, though at present they could not be seen, yet it was not long before that they were heard off, and felt too. For in a very short time *[in January 1676, the Susquehannocks]* had, in a most inhumane manner, murdered no less than 60 innocent people, no ways guilty of any actual injury done to these ill disarming, brutish heathen. By the blood of these poor souls, they thought that the wandering ghosts of those their Commissioners, before mentioned, might be atoned, and laid down to take their repose in the dismal shades of death, and they, at present, not obliged for to prosecute any further revenge. Therefore to prove whether the English was as ready for a peace, as themselves, they send in their remonstrance in the name of their Chief, (taken by an English interpreter,) unto the Governour of Virginia, with whom he expostulates in this sort. What was it that moved him to take up Arms, against him, his professed friend, in the behalf of the Marylanders, his professed enemies, contrary to that league made between [him] and himself? Declares as well his own as subjects grief to find the Virginians, of Friends, without any cause given, to become his foes, and to be so eager in their groundless quarrell, as to pursue the chase into another's dominions: Complains, that his messengers of peace, were not only murdered by the English, but the fact countenanced by the Governor's Connivance: For which, seeing no other ways to be satisfied, he had revenged himself, by killing 10 for one of the Virginians, such being the disproportion between his great men murdered, and those, by his command, slain. That now, this being done, if that his honour would allow him a valuable satisfaction for the damage he had sustained by the war, and no more concern himself in the Marylanders quarrel, he was content to renew and confirm the ancient league of amity; other ways himself, and those whom he had engaged to his interest (and their owne) were resalued to fight it out to the last man.

These proposals not being assented to by the English, as being derogatory and point blank, both to honour and intress, these Indians draw in others (formerly in subjection to the Virginians) to their aides: which being conjoined (in separate and united parties) they daily committed abundance of unguarded and unrevenged murders, upon the English; which they perpetrated in a most barbarous and horrid manner. By which means abundance of the frontier plantations became either depopulated by the Indians cruelties, or deserted by the planters fears, who were compelled to forsake there abodes, to find security for their lives; which they were not to part with, in the hands of the Indians, but under the worst of torments. For these brutish and inhumane brutes, least their cruelties might not be thought cruel enough, they devised a hundred ways to torture and torment those poor souls with, whose reached fate it was to fall in to their unmerciful hands. For some, before that they would deprive them of their lives, they would take a great deal of time to deprive them first of their skins, and if that life had not, through the anguish of their pain, forsaken there tormented bodies, they [with] their teeth (or some instrument,) tear the nails of [their fingers and their] toes, which put the poor sufferer to a woeful condition. One was prepared for the flames at James Towne, who endured much, but found means to escape....

And now it was that the poor distressed and doubly afflicted Planters began to curse and execrate that ill managed business at the Fort. Their cries were reiterated again and again, both to God and man for relief. But no appearance of long wish'd for safety arising in the Horizon of their hopes, they were ready, could they have told which way, to leave all and forsake the Colony; rather than to stay and be expos'd to the cruelties of the barbarous heathen.

SUPPLEMENTAL TEXTS

The following documents were written after the events of Bacon's Rebellion and are for use when the game is completed or at whatever point seems appropriate to the course instructor.

"A True Narrative of the Late Rebellion in Virginia, by the Royal Commissioners" (1677)

In September 1676 news of Bacon's uprising reached England. The Crown immediately dispatched a force of soldiers to suppress the rebellion and a royal commission to investigate it. The king also ordered that Governor Berkeley be removed from office and recalled him to London. In February 1677 the commissioners, their assistants, and several hundred royal troops arrived in Virginia. The commissioners received petitions of grievances, sworn testimony from private citizens, and reports from local officials. The final report, "A True Narrative of the Late Rebellion in Virginia, by the Royal Commissioners," excerpted here was presented to the king's privy council in October 1677.

Source: *Virginia Magazine of History and Biography* 4, no. 2 (October 1896): 117–54.

In July, 1675, certain Doegs and Susquehannock Indians on the Mary-land side, stealing some hogs from the English at Potomac, on the Virginia shore (as the River divides the same), were pursued by the English in a boat, beaten or killed and the hogs retaken from them; whereupon the Indians repairing to their Towne, report it to their Superiors, and how that one Mathew (whose hogs they had taken) had before abused and cheated them, in not paying them for such Indian truce as he had formerly bought of them, and that they took his hogs for satisfaction. Upon this (to be revenged on Mathews) an Indian war Captain, with some Indians, came over to Potomac and killed two of Mathew's servants, and came also a second time and killed his son.

[In September 1675, Col. Mason and a thousand Virginians trapped the Susquehannocks in an Indian fortress across the Potomac River in Maryland and laid siege to it.] . . . The Indians sent out 5 great men to Treaty of Peace, who were not Permitted to return to the Fort, but being kept prisoners some time were at last murdered by the English. . . .

At length (whether through negligence or cowardice) the Indians made their escape through the English, with all their wives, children and goods of value, wounding and killing some at their sally and going off. . . .

But about the beginning of January 1675-6, a Party of those abused Susquehannocks in Revenge of the Maryland business came suddenly down upon the weak Plantations at the head of Rappahannock and Potomac and killed at one time 36 persons and then immediately (as their custom is) ran off into the woods.

Noe sooner was this Intelligence brought to the Governor but he immediately called a court and ordered a competent force of horse and foot to pursue the Murderers under the Command of Sir Henry Chicheley and some other Gentlemen of the County of Rappahannock, giving them full Power by Commission to make Peace or War. But the men being ready to march out upon this Service the Governor on a sudden recalls this commission, Causes the men to be disbanded, and without any effectual course being taken for present Preservation, refers all to the next assembly; in the meantime, leaving the poor inhabitants under continual and deadly fears and terrors of their Lives.

Edward Randolph, "The Causes and Results of King Philip's War" (1685)

Edward Randolph was an emissary of King James II, sent to the colonies to investigate the violations of the Crown's colonial laws (that is, the Navigation Acts) and the overall state of colonial affairs, especially in New England. The selection below is Randolph's account of the war between the New England colonists and the American Indians in that region, led by Metacom (or Metacomet, who was called King Philip by the English).

As a report by a government official investigating affairs several years after the event, we have elected to include this among the Supplemental Texts.

Source: Albert Bushnell Hart, ed., *American History Told by Contemporaries*, vol. 1 (New York: Macmillan, 1898), 458–60.

What has been the original cause of the present war with the natives. What are the advantages or disadvantages arising thereby and will probably be the End?

Various are the reports and conjectures of the causes of the present Indian war. Some impute it to an imprudent zeal in the magistrates of Boston to christianize those heathen before they were civilized and injoyning them the strict observation of their laws, which, to a people so rude and licentious, hath proved even intolerable, and that the more, for that while the magistrates, for their profit, put the lawes severely in execution against the Indians, the people, on the other side, for lucre and gain, entice and provoke the Indians to the breach thereof, especially to drunkenness, to which those people are so generally addicted that they will strip themselves to their skin to have their fill of rum and brandy, the Massachusets having made a law that every Indian drunk should pay 10s. or be whipped, according to the discretion of the magistrate. Many of these poor people willingly offered their backs to the lash to save their money; whereupon, the magistrates finding much trouble and no profit to arise to the government by whipping, did change that punishment into 10 days work for such as could not or would not pay the fine of 10s. which did highly incense the Indians.

Some believe there have been vagrant and Jesuitical priests, who have made it their business, for some years past, to go from Sachem to Sachem, to exasperate the Indians against the English and to bring them into a confederacy, and that they were promised supplies from France and other parts to extirpate the English nation out of the continent of America. Others impute the cause to some injuries offered to the Sachim Philip; for he being possessed of a tract of land called Mount Hope, a very fertile, pleasant and rich soyle, some English had a mind to dispossess him thereof, who never wanting one pretense or other to attain their end, complained of injuries done by Philip and his Indians to their stock and cattle, whereupon Philip was often summoned before the magistrate, sometimes imprisoned, and never released but upon parting with a considerable part of his land.

But the government of the Massachusetts (to give it in their own words) do declare these are the great evils for which God hath given the heathen commission to rise against them: The woeful breach of the 5th commandment, in contempt of their authority, which is a sin highly provoking to the Lord: For men wearing long hair and periwigs made of women's hair; for women wearing borders of hair and for cutting, curling and laying out the hair, and disguising themselves by following strange fashions in their apparel: For profaneness in the people not frequenting their meetings, and others going away before the blessing be pronounced: For suffering the Quakers to live amongst them and to set up their thresholds by Gods thresholds, contrary to their old laws and resolutions.

With many such reasons, but whatever be the cause, the English have contributed much to their misfortunes, for they first taught the Indians the use of armes, and admitted them to be present at all their musters and trainings, and showed them how to handle, mend and fix their muskets, and have been furnished with all sorts of arms by permission of the government, so that the Indians are become excellent firemen. And at Natick there was a gathered church of praying Indians, who were exercised as trained bands, under officers of their own; these have been the most barbarous and cruel enemies to the English of any others. Capt. Tom, their leader, being lately taken and hanged at Boston, with one other of their chiefs.

That notwithstanding the ancient law of the country, made in the year 1633, that no person should sell any arms or ammunition to any Indian upon penalty of £10 for every gun, £5 for a pound of powder, and 40s. for a pound of shot, yet the government of the Massachusetts in the year 1657, upon designs to monopolize the whole Indian trade did publish and declare that the trade of furs and peltry with the Indians in their jurisdiction did solely and properly belong to their commonwealth and not to every indifferent person, and did enact that no person should trade with the Indians for any sort of peltry, except such as were authorized by that court, under the penalty of £100 for every offense, giving liberty to all such as should have license from them to sell, unto any Indian, guns, swords, powder and shot, paying to the treasurer 3d. for each gun and for each dozen of swords; 6d. for a pound of powder and for every ten pounds of shot, by which means the Indians have been abundantly furnished with great store of arms and ammunition to the utter ruin and undoing of many families in the neighboring colonies to enrich some few of their relations and church members.

No advantage but many disadvantages have arisen to the English by the war, for about 600 men have been slain, and 12 captains, most of them brave and stout persons and of loyal principles, whilst the church members had liberty to stay at home and not hazard their persons in the wilderness.

The loss to the English in the several colonies, in their habitations and stock, is reckoned to amount to £150,000 there having been about 1200 houses burned, 8000 head of cattle, great and small, killed, and many thousand bushels of wheat, peas and other grain burned (of which the Massachusetts colony hath not been damnified one third part, the great loss falling upon New Plymouth and Connecticut colonies) and upward of 3000 Indians men women and children destroyed, who if well managed would have been very serviceable to the English, which makes all manner of labor dear.

The war at present is near an end. In Plymouth colony the Indians surrender themselves to Gov. Winslow, upon mercy, and bring in all their arms, are wholly at his disposal, except life and transportation; but for all such as have been notoriously cruel to women and children, so soon as discovered they are to be executed in the sight of their fellow Indians.

The government of Boston has concluded a peace upon these terms.

1. That there be henceforward a firm peace between the Indians and English.
2. That after publication of the articles of peace by the general court, if any English shall willfully kill an Indian, upon due proof, he shall die, and if an Indian kill an Englishman and escape, the Indians are to produce him, and lie to pass trial by the English laws.

That the Indians shall not conceal any known enemies to the English, but shall discover them and bring them to the English.

That upon all occasions the Indians are to aid and assist the English against their enemies, and to be under English command.

Robert Beverley, *The History and Present State of Virginia* (1705)

This retrospective on Bacon's Rebellion was written by the son of Maj. Robert Beverley, who was a staunch supporter of the governor.

What evidence can you find of the author sharing a pro-Berkeley bias with his father? How does this account compare with the events as they unfolded in your game experience?

Source: Robert Beverley, *The History and Present State of Virginia*, ed. Susan Scott Parrish (Chapel Hill: University of North Carolina Press, 2013), 56–60.

The occasion of this Rebellion is not easy to be discovered. But 'tis certain that there were many things that concurred towards it. For it cannot be imagined, that upon the Instigation of Two or Three Traitors, as some pretend to say, the whole Country would have fallen into so much distraction; in which People did not only hazard their Necks by Rebellion: But endeavored to ruin a Governor, whom they all entirely loved and had unanimously chosen; a Gentleman who had devoted his whole Life and Estate to the Service of his Country; and against whom in Thirty Five Years' Experience there had never been one single Complaint. . . . So that in all Probability there was something else in the Wind, without which the Body of the Country [would have] never been engaged in that Insurrection.

Four things may be reckoned to have been the main Ingredients towards this intestine Commotion. First, the extreme low Price of Tobacco, and the ill usage of the Planters in the Exchange of Goods for it, which the Country, with all their earnest Endeavors, could not remedy. Secondly, the Splintering [of] the Colony into [numerous] Proprieties, contrary to the original Charters; and the extravagant taxes [many colonists] were forced to undergo, to relieve themselves from those Grants. Thirdly, the heavy restraints and Burdens laid upon their Trade by Act of Parliament in England. Fourthly, the Disturbance given by the Indians. . . .

This addition of mischief *[Indian attacks on white frontier settlements]* to minds already full of discontent, made people ready to vent all their resentment against the poor Indians. There was nothing to be got by Tobacco; neither could they turn any other manufacture to advantage; so that most of the poorer Sort were willing to quit their unprofitable employments, and go volunteers against the Indians.

At first they flocked together tumultuously, running in Troops from one Plantation to another without a Head; till at last the seditious humor of Colonel [sic] Nath. Bacon, led him to be of the Party. This Gentleman had been brought up at one of the Inns of Court in England, and had a moderate Fortune. He was young, bold, active, of an inviting Aspect, and powerful Elocution. In a Word, he was every way qualified to head a giddy and unthinking Multitude. Before he had been Three Years in the Country, he was, for his extraordinary Qualifications, made one of the Council, and in great Honour and Esteem among the People. For this Reason he no sooner gave Countenance to this riotous Mob, but they all presently fixed their Eyes upon him for their General, and accordingly made their Addresses to him. As soon as he found this, he *[berated them]* publicly. He aggravated the Indian mischiefs, complaining, that they were occasioned for want of due regulation of the trade. He recounted particularly the other grievances and pressures they lay under; and pretended that he accepted their command with no other Intention, but to do them and the country service, in which he was willing to encounter the greatest difficulties and dangers. He further assured them, he would never lay down his arms, till he had revenged their sufferings upon the Indians, and redressed all their other grievances.

"The History of Bacon's and Ingram's Rebellion in Virginia, and in 1676"

See introductory notes above. This is the continuation of that account as it relates to the events covered during game play.

At last it was concluded [in March 1676], as a good expedient for to put the country in to some degree of safety, for to plant Forts upon the Frontiers, thinking thereby to put a stop unto the Indians excursions: which after the expense of a great deal of time and charge, being finished, came short of the designed ends.

For the Indians quickly found out where about these mouse traps were set, and for what purpose, and so resolved to keep out of there danger; which they might easily enough do, without any detriment to their designs. For though here by they were compelled (tis possible) to go a little about, yet they never thought; much of their labor, so long as they were not debarred from doing of mischief; which was not in the power of these forts to prevent: For if that the English did, at any time, know that there was more ways in to the wood then one, to kill deer, the Indians found more than a thousand out of the wood, to kill men, and not come near the danger of the forts neither.

Elizabeth Bacon, Letter to Her Sister in London (June 29, 1676)

Elizabeth Bacon's letter offers an insider's perspective on the conditions at the "frontier." Although her bias as Nathaniel Bacon's wife cannot be avoided, her private letter provides a rare glimpse from a woman's perspective into the challenges facing Anglo-Virginians along the edge of European settlement.

What does this letter reveal that was not already apparent about conditions in the backcountry, popular support for Bacon, and other related issues?

In what ways does her perspective as a woman come through in the document?

Source: "Bacon's Rebellion," *William and Mary Quarterly* 9, no. 1 (July 1900): 1–10.

Dear Sister,

I pray God keep the worst Enemy I have from ever being in such a sad condition as I have been in since my [previous letter to you], occasioned by the troublesome Indians, who have killed one of our Overseers at an outward plantation which we had, and we have lost a great stock of cattle, which we had upon it, and a good crop that we should have made there, such plantation Nobody durst come nigh, which is a very great loss to us.

If you had been here, it would have grieved your heart to hear the pitiful complaints of the people, the Indians killing the people daily, the Governor not taking any notice of it for to hinder them, but let them daily do all the mischief they can; I am sure if the Indian were not cowards, they might have destroyed all the upper plantations and killed all the people upon them; the Governor so much their friend, that he would not suffer any body to hurt one of the Indians; the poor people came to your brother to desire him to help against the Indians, and he being very much concerned for the loss of his Overseer, and for the loss of so many men and women and children's lives every day, he was willing to do them all the good he could; so he begged of the Governor for a commission in several letters to him, that

CORE TEXTS 87

he might go out against them, but he would not grant one, so daily more mischief done by them, so your brother not able to endure any longer, he went out without a commission. The Governor being very angry with him put out high things against him, and told me that he would most certainly hang him as soon as he returned. . . . The fight [with the Indians] did continue nigh a night and a day without any intermission. They did destroy a great many of the Indians, thanks be to God, and might have killed a great many more, but the Governor were so much the Indians' friend and our enemy, that he sent the Indians word that Mr. Bacon was out against them that they might save themselves.

Philip Ludwell, "An Account of the Rebellious Mutiny Raised by Nathanial Bacon" (1676)

Philip Ludwell, another of Governor Berkeley's close supporters, reports on the origins of the rebellion. Writing to Sir Joseph Williamson, the foreign affairs secretary in the royal cabinet, Ludwell says little about the course of the uprising through the summer but dwells instead on an explanation of how Bacon came to rebel against the governor.

What does Ludwell say about Bacon? How does he describe him? How does that compare with his assessment of Berkeley?

Source: British National Archives, Colonial State Papers, CO 1/37, no. 16.

Account of the distressed condition of this poor country both from the Indians and the rebellious mutiny raised by Nathaniel Bacon, which has come "to that prodigious height that indeed I think no story either ancient or modern can out-do, blood only excepted." Has not yet been two days out of durance, where the Governor, Council, and Burgesses, with divers others were strictly kept by Bacon and about 500 of the scum of the country three days until he had obtained his most unreasonable and illegal demands. Relates the proceedings of the Assembly in March last to take the best means to destroy their Indian enemies by erecting forts at the head of each river until an army could be raised, but while this was in action, Bacon, "a man of little above one year's experience in the country," infused into the people the vast charge this would bring on them, and gathered about him a rabble of the basest sort, and with them began to stand at defiance against the Government. Being "pleasant and sympathetic with the humors," in an instant he infected almost every corner of the country.

The Governor perceiving the disease to grow dangerous and by its spreading the cure difficult used all possible means to reclaim Bacon from his mutinous ways, but he still proceeded contrary to positive order and command. His first exploit was to seize two Indians who had always lived in friendship with the English, these he put to death with much horror and cruelty without examining their crime, and drove our neighbor friendly Indians away, who are as necessary to us as dogs to hunt wolves. Hardly 100 friendly Indians on all our borders, and at least 1,500 enemies who continually prey upon our frontier plantations.

Bacon's march with about 300 to the Occaneeches who live on an island 150 miles from the falls of James River, the march of the Occaneeches and assault of a fort of the Susquehanna's which they destroyed and brought back six Mannakin Indians and seven Indians prisoners and the plunder to Bacon who tortured the prisoners to death. Dispute between Persicles, King of the Occaneeches, and Bacon as to division of the plunder, which ended in a fight in which Persicles and 40 or 50 of his Indians were killed, and 16 or 17 of Bacon's men.

Bacon then made a hasty retreat, and on his return the Governor again ordered him to lay down his arms, and then was forced to publicly declare him a rebel; but Bacon with 40 armed men came to the Court House and commanded the Sheriff to forbear publishing the Governor's declaration, threatening him terribly if he proceeded, and being the day of election of Burgesses, Bacon was by his ruling party chosen a Burgess. On 5th June the Assembly were to meet at James City, and the next day Bacon came down the river in a sloop with about 50 armed men and in the night landed at Sandy Bay, half-a-mile off, where he held a private conference with one Lawrence and one Drummond about three hours and then went to their boats. But they were discovered; an alarm was given and armed boats sent in pursuit, and about three in the afternoon Bacon was taken and brought to town with his men, who were kept guarded, but Bacon released on his parole.

After which in open Court he made a full and free submission to the Government and engaged his honor and estate never to do the like, but to use his utmost endeavors to allay the commotions. He was again sworn of the Council and promised a Commission to raise volunteers against the Indians, but instead of performing his obligations he raised new and heightened the old commotions, got at several places about 500 men, "whose fortunes and inclinations were equally desperate," and with these marched towards the town, which on 23rd June he entered, there being no force to resist him, and drew up his men before the State House, where the Governor, Council, and Burgesses were sitting.

After sending out his guards to secure all parts, the Governor sent two of the Council to know what they came for, Bacon replied for a Commission; account of what took place, his refusing the Governor's Commission to be "Commander-in-Chief of all the volunteer soldiers to go against the Indians" and his demand to be "General of all the forces in Virginia against the Indians," the Governor's reply that he would rather have both his hands cut off than grant such a Commission, and challenge to Bacon to decide the controversy with the sword; Bacon's refusal and threats to the Burgesses in the State House where 100 guns ready cocked were presented at them, saying that he would pull down the house and have their blood, with such dreadful new coined oaths "as if he thought God was delighted with his ingenuity in that kind." The House demanded a little respite and supplicated the Governor to grant the commission in Bacon's form, which was done, and other propositions and demands, very hard ones, were granted, having upon us the expectation of having all our throats cut and the fear of the Indians.

The laws of Assembly were sent out to the people to be read, but they rose up like a swarm of bees and swore they would hear no laws nor have any but what they pleased. On Sunday 25th June news came that the Indians had murdered eight of our people, in two places. The Governor sent to call the House together, and desired Sir Henry Chicheley to see Bacon and demand what he intended, that either he should march away to secure the people from the Indians or suffer us to go to our respective countries that a force might be immediately raised to suppress these Indians.

The Assembly was then dissolved, but Bacon refused to let the Governor go home to see his family until the next morning, when Bacon marched out of town, "by which all were released from their durance." They have marched to where the last mischief was done, but doubts not they will soon hear of him again. Entreats him to be as he doubts not these agents will be a mediator to the King for this poor languishing country.

Thomas Ludwell and Robert Smith, "Proposals for Reducing the Rebels in Virginia to Their Obedience" (1676)

Unbeknownst to the residents of Virginia at the time, the reports received in England of the rebellion led to relatively swift action in the upper echelons of the British government. Thomas Ludwell was formerly secretary of the colony and the brother of Philip Ludwell, who replaced him as secretary in 1675, when Thomas returned to England to represent the burgesses to the Crown. In October 1676, Thomas recommended decisive action in Virginia to restore order and bring most of the colony's population back into a state of loyalty to the king. His pro-Berkeley bias is apparent throughout.

What does he consider the ultimate source of discontent in the colony?

Source: British National Archives, Colonial State Papers, CO 1/38, no. 18.

Proposals, most humbly offered to his most sacred Majesty by Thomas Ludwell and Robert Smith, for the reducing the Rebels in Virginia to their obedience. It being evidently true that that Colony has always been and in the worst of times eminently loyal to the Crown of England, they cannot believe that the present disorders have their beginning from disaffection to his Majesty or his government either here or there, or that the infection hath seized upon any of the better or more industrious sort of people, but from the poverty and uneasiness of some of the meanest, whose discontents render them easy to be misled, and, as they believe this to be the sole cause of these troubles, so are confident that, upon the first appearance of his Majesty's resentment of their disobedience and commands on all his subjects to return to their duty, there will be a speedy separation of the sound parts from the rabble, and many who now follow Bacon, out of opinion that they do his Majesty and the country service against the Indians, will quit the party when they understand it to be rebellion, and the hands of those who abhor the present disaffection will be strengthened by his Majesty's resolution of vindicating his authority and punishing the principal offenders against it.

To effect which they suggest two ways: either to send a force superior to any that can be brought against it, or a smaller number of men to assist those ready to obey his Majesty's commands. Also, that it will be for his Majesty's service that his Majesty's authority be justified in the person of Sir W. Berkeley before his removal from the government, for the reasons given. That a frigate proceeds directly to James Town able to land 200 men. Suggestions for taking or killing Bacon, and the prevention of further mischiefs by him or his assistants. And that the Lords Proprietors of Maryland be commanded not to receive any inhabitants of Virginia. Offer for consideration, as the most effectual means to reduce Virginia to a lasting obedience, that those grants which have and still do so much disturb their minds may be taken in, and their just privileges and properties settled for the future on a solid foundation, the fear of forfeiting which would keep them in perpetual awe.

King Charles II, "A Proclamation for the Suppressing of a Rebellion Lately Raised Within the Plantation of Virginia" (1676)

After hearing reports of the disorder in Virginia and receiving recommendations from advisors, King Charles II instituted the following policy on October 26, clearly assuming that Bacon was at fault and needed to be apprehended and the rebellion put down. Ironically, on this very date, Bacon died of typhoid in the colony. Although the rebellion continued under the leadership of John Ingram, Berkeley's counteroffensive changed the tide of the war. By the time the royal commissioners arrived in Virginia, the rebellion had collapsed.

Source: British National Archives, Colonial State Papers, CO 1/38, nos. 7–9; see also CO 5/1355, pp. 129–32, and CO 389/6, pp. 140–44.

Whereas Nathaniel Bacon, the younger, of the Plantation of Virginia, and others his adherents and accomplices, being persons of mean and desperate fortunes, have lately in a traitorous and rebellious manner levied war within the said Plantation against the King, and more particularly being assembled in warlike manner to the number of about 500 persons, did, in June last, besiege the Governor and Assembly, and by menaces and threats of present death compel said Governor and Assembly to pass divers pretended Acts. To the end that said Nathaniel Bacon and his accomplices may suffer such punishment as they justly deserve, his Majesty doth declare that said Nathaniel Bacon and all his Majesty's subjects as have taken arms under and assisted or shall hereafter take arms or assist said Nathaniel Bacon in carrying on the war shall be guilty of high treason. And his Majesty strictly commands his loving subjects to use their utmost endeavors to secure the persons of the said Nathaniel Bacon and his accomplices in order to bring them to their legal trial.

And his Majesty doth declare that such person or persons as shall apprehend said Nathaniel Bacon shall have a reward from his Majesty's royal bounty of 300*L*. sterling, to be paid in money by the Lieutenant-Governor. And because many of Bacon's adherents may have been seduced by him into this rebellion by false pretenses, his Majesty doth declare that if within twenty days of the publishing this Proclamation any such adherent submits himself to his Majesty's government, and takes the oath of obedience and gives security for his future good behavior, such person is hereby pardoned: but those who shall not accept this offer of pardon, but persist in said rebellion, their servants or slaves as shall take arms under his Majesty's Governor or Commander-in-Chief shall have their liberty and be forever free from the service of said offenders.

And that his Majesty's loving subjects may understand how careful his Majesty is to remove all just grievances, he hath not only given instructions to reduce the salaries of the Members of the Assembly to such moderate rates as may render them less burthensome to the country, but hath also sent Herbert Jeffreys, Sir John Berry, and Francis Moryson, his Majesty's Commissioners, to inquire into and report to his Majesty all such other grievances as his Majesty's subjects within said Plantation do at present lie under, to the end such redress and relief may be made as shall be agreeable to his Majesty's royal wisdom and compassion. And his Majesty hereby declares that the pretended Acts and Laws made in the Assembly held at James city in June last shall be null and void.

Royal Commissioners' Narrative (1677)

The Royal Commissioners arrived in Virginia expecting an ongoing war and were surprised to find it was all over. They also discovered that circumstances were more complicated than they had been led to believe before leaving England. Below is an excerpt from their report in which they include a petition of grievance from the citizens of Isle of Wight County, May 1677. The residents there were troubled by Berkeley's administration and found Bacon a sympathetic leader.

What is the issue that they raise? How does this concern compare with the assessment of Bacon's followers by the pro-Berkeley writers above?

Source: British National Archives, Colonial State Papers, CO 1/39 ff.257.

... We having a long time lain under great oppressions, and every year being more and more oppressed with great taxes, and still do load us with greater and unnecessary burdens; it was enacted by the Governor and assembly for the building of forts back in the woods upon several great men's Lands, under pretense of security for us against the Indians, which we perceiving and well knowing that their pretense was no security for us, but rather a ruin to the country, which was the cause of our [up]rising with intents to have our taxes Lowered, not that we rose in any ways of Rebellion against our most [dear] Sovereign Lord the King as by our actions may appear, for we no sooner rose. But we sent in a petition our grievance to Sir William Berkeley, who was not at home but the Lady Berkeley promised that she would acquaint his Honor with our business, and by her request or command, we every man returned home. . . .

Anna Cotton, "An Account of Our Late Troubles in Virginia" (1676)

Anna Cotton, wife to John Cotton, was apparently well educated and highly literate, especially compared to most women of the colony. Her account is likely a shortened version of one written by her husband and sent to a family friend in England. The Cottons were personally acquainted with some of the protagonists of this game and were contemporaries to the tragic events that unfolded in the colony. It is as close to an eyewitness account as any other text but was not made public until published in 1804.

Unlike some of the more polemical accounts, Cotton's report attempts to give a broad perspective on the events. Certainly, it is quite detailed and helps broaden the narrative as told by Bacon's and Berkeley's supporters.

What information does this account provide that is omitted in earlier ones?

Source: *Richmond Enquirer,* September 12, 1804 (repr., Washington, DC: Peter Force, 1835).

To Mr. C. H. at Yardley in Northamptonshire.

Sir, I having seen yours directed to——and considering that you cannot have your desires satisfied that way, for the aforementioned reasons, I have by his permission, adventured to send you this brief account, of those affaires, so far as I have been informed.

The Susquehanians and Marylanders of friends being engaged enemies (as hath by former letter bin hinted to you) and that the Indians being resolutely bent not to forsake there forte; it came to this pointe, yet the Marylanders were obliged (finding themselves too weak to do the work themselves) to supplicate (too soon granted) aide of the Virginians, put under the conduct of one Colonel Washington (him whom you have sometimes seen at your house) who being joined with the Marylanders, invests the Indians in there forte, with a negligent siege; upon which the enemy made several salleys, with as many losses to the besiegers; and at last gave them the opportunity to desert the Fort, after that the English had (contrary to ye law of arms) beat out the brains of 6 great men sent out to treaty a peace: an action of ill consequence, as it proved after. For the Indians having in the dark, slipped through the Legure, and in their passage knocked 10 of the besiegers on the head, which they found fast asleep, leaving the rest to prosecute the siege, (as Scoging's Wife brooding the Eggs which the Fox had sucked) they resolved to employ there liberty in avenging their Commissioners blood, which they speedily effected in the death of sixty innocent souls, and then send in their Remonstrance to the Governor, in justification of the fact, with this expostulation annexed: Demanding what it was moved him to take up arms against them, his professed friends, in the behalf of the Marylanders, there avowed enemies. Declaring their sorrow to see the Virginians, of friends to become such violent enemies as to pursue the Chase in to another's dominions.

Complains that their messengers sent out for peace were not only knocked on the head but the fact countenanced by the governor; for which (finding no other way to be satisfied) they had revenged themselves, by killing ten for one of the English; such being the disproportion between there men murdered, and those by them slain, there's being persons of quality, the other of inferior Ranke: Professing that if they may have a valuable satisfaction, for the damage they had sustained by the English, and that the Virginians would with-draw their aides from the Marylanders quarrel; that then they would renew the league with Sir William Berkeley other ways they would prosecute the war to the last man; and the hardest fend off.

This was fair play, from fowl gamesters. But the proposals not to be allowed of as being contrary to the honor of the English, the Indians proceeds, and having drawn the neighboring Indians into their aid, in a short time, they commit abundance of unguarded and unrevenged murders; by which means a great many of the outward plantations were deserted; the doing whereof did not only terrify the whole colony, but supplanted those esteems the people had formerly for Sir William Berkeley whom they judged too remiss in applying means to stop the fury of the Heathen; and to settle their affections, and expectations, upon one Esqr. Bacon, newly come into the Country, one of the Council, and nearly related to your late wives father-in-law, whom they desired might be commissioned General, for the Indian war; Which Sr. William (for some reasons best known unto himself) denying, the Gent: man (without any scruple) accepts of a commission from the peoples affections, signed by the emergences of affairs and the Country's danger; and so forth with advanced with a small party (composed of such that own his authority) against the Indians; on whom, it is said he did signal execution: In his absence he and those with him, were declared Rebels to the State, May 29, and forces raised to reduce him to his obedience; at the head of which the Governor advanced, some 30 or 40 miles to find Bacon out, but not knowing which way he was gone, he dismissed his army, retiring himself and council, to James Towne, there to be ready for the assembly, which was now upon the point of meeting: Whether Bacon, some few days after his return home from his Indian march, prepared to render an account of his service; for which himself and most of those with him in the expedition, were imprisoned; from whence they were freed by a judgment in court upon Bacon's trial, himself readmitted into the council and promised a commission the Monday following (this was on the Saturday) against the Indians; with which deluded, he smothers his resentments, and begs leave to visit his Lady (now sick, as he pretended) which granted, he returns to Towne at the head of 4 or 5 hundred men, well-armed: reassumes his demands for a commission.

Which, after some howlers struggling with the Governor, being obtained, according to his desire, he takes order for the country's security, against the attempts of skulking Indians; fills up his numbers and provisions, according to the gage of his commission; and so once more advanced against the Indians, who hearing of his approaches, calls in their runners and scouts, be taking themselves to be there subterfuges and lurking holes. The General (for so he was now denominated) had not reached the head of York River, but that a Post overtakes him, and informs, that Sir William Berkeley was a raising the Trained-bands in Gloucester, with an intent, either to fall into his rear, or otherways to cut him off when he should return weary and spent from his Indian service. This strange news put him, and those with him, shrewdly to their triumphs, believing that a few such deals or shuffles (call them what you will) might quickly ring both cards and game out of his hands. He saw that there was an absolute necessity of destroying the Indians, and that there was some care to be taken for his own and Army's safety, other-ways the work might happen to be wretchedly done, where the laborers were made cripples, and be compelled (instead of a sword) to make use of a crutch. It vexed him to the heart (as he said) to think, that while he was a hunting Wolves, tigers and bears, which daily destroyed our harmless and innocent Lambs, that he, and those with him, should be pursued in the rear with a full cry, as more savage beasts.

He perceived like the corn, he was light between those stones which might grind him to powder; if he did not look the better about him. For the preventing of which, after a short consult with his officers, he countermarched his Army (about 500 in all) down to the Middle Plantation: of which the Governor being informed, ships himself and adherers, for Accomack (for the Gloucester men refused to own his quarrel against the General) after he had caused Bacon, in these parts to be proclaimed a Rebel once more, July 29.

Bacon being sat down with his Army at the Middle Plantation, sends out an invitation unto all the prime Gent: men in these parts, to give him a meeting in his quarters, there to consult how the Indians were to be proceeded against, and himself and Army protected against the designs of Sir William Berkeley against whose Papers, of the 29 of May, and his Proclamation since, he puts forth his Replication and those papers upon these dilemmas.

First, whether persons wholly devoted to the King and country, haters of sinister and by-respects, adventuring their lives and fortunes, to kill and destroy all in Arms, against King and country; that never plotted, contrived, or indevoured the destruction, detriment or wrong of any of his Majesties subjects, their lives, fortunes, or estates can deserve the names of Rebels and Traitors: secondly he cites his own and solders peaceable behavior, calling the whole country to witness against him if they can; he upbraids some in authority with the meanness of their parts, others now rich with the meanness of their estates, when they came into the country, and questions by what just ways they have obtained there wealth; whether they have not been the sponges that hath sucked up the public treasury: Questions what arts, sciences, schools of Learning, or manufactories, have been promoted in authority: Justifies his aversions, in general against the Indians; upbraids the Governor for maintaining there quarrel, though never so unjust, against the Christians rights; his refusing to admit an English man's oath against an Indian, when that Indians bare word should be accepted of against an Englishman: said something against the Governor concerning the Beaver trade, as not in his power to dispose of to his own profit, it being a Monopoly of the crown; Questions whether the Traders at the heads of the Rivers being his Factors, do not buy and sell the blood of their brethren and country men, by furnishing the Indians with powder, shot and fire arms, contrary to the laws of the colony: He arraigns one Colonel Cowells assertion, for saying that the English are bound to protect the Indians, to the hazard of their blood. And so concludes with an Appeal to the King and Parliament, where he doubts not but that his and the peoples cause will be impartially heard.

To comply with the Generals invitation, hinted in my former letter, there was a great convention of the people met him in his quarters; the result of whose meeting was an engagement, for the people (of what quality so ever, excepting servants) to subscribe to consisting of 3 heads. First to be aiding, with their lives and estates, the General, in the Indian war: secondly, to oppose Sr. Williams designs, if he had any, to hinder the same: and lastly, to protect the General, Army and all that should subscribe this engagement, against any power that should be sent out of England, till it should be granted that the countries complaint might be heard, against Sr. William before the King and Parliament. These 3 heads being methodized, and put in to form, by the Clerk of the Assembly, who happened to be at this meeting, and read unto the people, held a dispute, from almost no one, till midnight, pro and con, whether the same might, in the last Article especially, be without danger taken. The General, and some others of the chief men was Resolute in the affirmative, asserting its innocence, and protesting, without it, he would surrender up his commission to the Assembly, and let them find other servants, to do the country's work: this, and the news, that the Indians were fallen down in to Gloucester county, and had killed some people about Carter's Creek; made the people willing to take the engagement. The chief men that subscribed it at this meeting, were coll. Swan, coll. Beale, coll. Ballard, Esq. Bray, (all four of the council) coll. Jordan, coll. Smith, of Purton, coll. Scarsbrook, coll. Miller, coll. Lawrane, and Mr. Drummond, late Governor of Carolina; all persons, with whom you have been formerly acquainted.

This work being over, and orders taken for an Assembly to sit down the 4 of September (the writs being issued out in his majesties name, and signed by 4 of the Council, before named) the General once more sits out to find the Indians: of which Sr. William have gained intelligence, to prevent Bacons designs by the Assembly, returns from Accomack, with about 1000 solders, and others, in 5 ships and 10 sloops to James town; in which was some 900 Baconians (for soe now they began to be called, for a mark of distinction) under the command of coll. Hansford, who was commissioned by Bacon, to raise Forces (if need were) in his absence, for the safety of the country. Unto these Sr. William sends in a summons for a Rendition of ye place, with a pardon to all that would decline Bacons and entertain his cause. What was returned to this summons I know not; but in the night the Baconians forsake the Towne, by the advice of Drummond and Lawrence (who were both excepted, in the Governors summons, out of mercy) every one returning to their own abodes, excepting Drummond, Hansford, Lawrence, and some few others, who goes to find out the General, now returned to the head of York River, having spent his provisions in following the Indians on whom he did sum execution, and sent them packing a great way from the Borders.

Before that Drummond and those with him had reached the General, he had dismissed his Army, to their respective habitations, to gather strength against the next intended expedition; accepting some few reserved for his Guard, and persons living in these parts; unto whom, those that came with Hansford being joined, made about 150 in all: With these Bacon, by a swift march, before any news was heard of his return from the Indians, in these parts, comes to Towne, to ye consternation of all in it, and there blocks the Governor up; which he easily effected by this unheard of project. He was no sooner arrived at Towne, but by several small parties of Horse (2 or 3 in a party, for more he could not spare) he fetched into his little League, all the prime men's wives, whose Husbands were with the Governor, (as coll. Bacons Lady, Madm. Bray, Madm. Page, Madm. Ballard, and others) which the next morning he presents to the view of their husbands and friends in town, upon the top of the small work he had cast up in the night; where he caused them to tarry till he had finished his defense against his enemies shot, it being the only place (as you do know well enough) for those in towne to make a salley at. Which when completed, and the Governor understanding that the Gentle women were withdrawn in to a place of safety, he sends out some 6 or 700 hundreds of his solders, to beat Bacon out of his Trench: But it seems that those works, which were protected by such charms (when a raising) that plugged up the enemies shot in their gains, could not now be stormed by a virtue less powerful (when finished) then the sight of a few white Aprons: otherways the service had been more honorable and the damage less, several of those who made the salley being slain and wounded, without one drop of Blood drawn from the enemy.

Within two or three days after this disaster, the Governor reships himself, solders, and all the inhabitants of the town, and their goods: and so to Accomack again; leaving Bacon to enter the place at his pleasure, which he did the next morning before day, and the night following burns it down to the ground to prevent a future siege, as he said. Which Flagrant, and Flagitious Act performed, he draws his men out of town, and marched them over York River, at Tindells point, to find out Colonel Brent, who was advancing fast upon him, from Potomac, at the head of 1200 men, (as he was informed) with a design to raise Bacons siege, from before the town, or other ways to fight him, as he saw cause.

But, Brent's shoulders no sooner heard that Bacon was got on the north-side Yorke River, with an intent to fight them, and that he had beat the Governor out of the town, and fearing, if he met with them, that he might beat them out of their lives they basely forsake there colors, the greater part adhering to Bacons cause; resolving with the Persians to go and worship the rising sun, now approaching near there Horizon: of which Bacon being informed, he stops his proceedings that way, and begins to provide for another expedition against the Indian, of whom he had heard no news since his last March, against them: which while he was a contriving, Death summons him to more urgent affairs in to whose hands (after a short siege) he surrenders his life, leaving his commission in the custody of his Lieut. General, one Ingram, newly coming to the country.

Sr. William no sooner had news that Bacon was Dead but he sends over a party, in a sloop to Yorke who snapped Colonel Hansford, and others with him, that keep a negligent guard at Colonel Reades house under his command: When Hansford came to Accomack, he had the honor to be the first Virginian

CORE TEXTS 95

born that ever was hanged; the solders (about 20 in all) that were taken with him, were committed to Prison. Capt. Carver, Capt. Wilford, Capt. Farloe, with 5 or 6 others of less note, taken at other places, ending their days as Hansford did; Major Cheesman being appointed, but it seems not designated to the like end, which he prevented by dying in prison through ill usage, as it is said.

This execution being over (which the Baconians termed cruelty in the abstract) Sr. William ships himself and solder for York River, casting Anchor at Tindells point; from whence he sends up a hundred and 20 men to surprise a Gard, of about, 30 men and boys, kept at coll. Bacons house under the command of Major Whaley; who being forewarned by Hansford fate, prevented the designed conflict with the death of the commander in chief, and the taking some prisoners: Major Lawrence Smith, with 600 men, meeting with the like fate at coll. Pates house, in Gloucester, against Ingram, (the Baconian General) only Smith saved himself, by leaving his men in the lurch, being all made prisoners; whom Ingram dismissed to their own homes; Ingram himself, and all under his command, within a few days after, being reduced to his duty, by the well contrivance of Capt. Grantham, who was now lately arrived in York River: which put a period to the war, and brought the Governor ashore at Col. Bacons, where he was presented with Mr. Drummond; taken the day before in Chickahominy swamp, half famished, as himself related to my Husband. From Col. Bacons, the next day, he was conveyed, in Irons to Mr. Brays (whither the Governor was removed) to his trial, where he was condemned within half an hour after his coming to Esqr. Brays, to be hanged at the Middle Plantation, within 4 hours after condemnation; where he was accordingly, executed, with a pitiful French man.

Which done, the Governor removes to his own house, to settle his and the countries repose, after his many troubles; which he effected by the advice of his council and an Assembly convened at the Greene Spring; where several were condemned to be executed, prime actors in ye Rebellion; as Esqr. Bland, coll. Cruse, and som other hanged at Bacons Trench; Capt. Yong, of Chickahominy, Mr. Hall, clerk of New-Kent court, James Wilson (once your servant) and one Leift. Colonel Page, (one that my Husband bought of Mr. Lee, when he kept store at your house) all four executed at coll. Reads, over against Tindells point; and Anthony Arnell (the same that did live at your house) hanged in chains at West point, besides several others executed on the other side James River: enough (they say in all) to outnumber those slain in the whole war; on both sides: it being observable that the sword was more favorable then the Halter, as there was a greater liberty taken to run from the sharpness of the one, then would be allowed to shun the dull embraces of the other: the Hangman being more dreadful to the Baconians, then their General was to the Indians: as it is counted more honorable, and less terrible, to dye like a solder, then to be hanged like a dog.

Thus Sr. have I rendered you an account of our late troubles in Virginia, which I have performed too wordishly; but I did not know how to help it; Ignorance in some cases is a prevalent overture in pleading for pardon, I hope mine may have the fortune to prove so in the behalf of

Sr. your friend and servant,
ANNA COTTON.
From Queen's Creek

Virginia Laws Regarding Labor, Slavery, and Race: Acts I, II, and X (1679–1682)

Note the ways in which racial attitudes among Anglo-Virginians developed since Bacon's Rebellion in these excerpts, further entrenching animosity for Native Americans and Afro-Virginians.

How do these laws compare with legislative actions taken by characters in your game? To what degree did the events of the war itself affect the judgment of your characters when they took these actions?

Source: William Waller Hening, ed., *The Statutes at Large; Being a Collection of the Laws of Virginia, From the First Session of the Legislature, in the Year 1619* (New York: R&W&G Bartow, 1823), 2:440, 481–82, 491–93.

At a Grand Assembly begun at James City the 25th of April, 1679:

Act II

. . . And for the better encouragement and more orderly government of the soldiers, that what Indian prisoners or other plunder shall be taken in war, shall be free purchase to the soldier taking the same. And where any difference shall happen among the soldiers in such or like matters, the same to be adjudged, decided, or determined by their respective chief commanders.[2]

At a General Assembly begun at James City the eight day of June, Anno 1680:

Act X

. . . Whereas the frequent meeting of considerable numbers of negro slaves under pretence of feasts and burials is judged of dangerous consequence; for prevention whereof for the future, Be it enacted by the kings most excellent majestie by and with the consent of the general assembly, and it is hereby enacted by the authority aforesaid, that from and after the publication of this law it shall not be lawful for any negro or other slave to carry or arm himself with any club, staff, gun, sword or any other weapon of defence or offence, nor to go or depart from of his masters ground without a certificate from his master, mistress or overseer, and such permission not to be granted but upon particuler and necessary occasions; and every negro or slave so offending not having a certificate as aforesaid shall be sent to the next constable, who is thereby enjoined and required to give the said negro twenty lashes on his bare back well laid on, and so sent home to his said master, mistress or overseer. And it is further enacted by the authority aforesaid that if any negro or other slave shall presume to lift up his hand in opposition against any Christian, shall for every such offence, upon due proof made thereof by the oath of the party before a magistrate, have and receive thirty lashes on his bare back well laid on. And it is hereby further enacted by the authority aforesaid that if any negro or other slave shall absent himself from his masters service and lye hid and lurking in obscure places, committing injuries to the inhabitants, and shall resist any person or persons that shall by any lawful authority be employed to apprehend and take the said negro, that then in case of such resistance, it shall be lawful for such person or persons to kill the said negro or slave so lying out and resisting, and that this law be once every six months published at the respective county courts and parish churches within this colony.

At a General Assembly begun at James City November the Tenth Anno Domini 1682:

Act I

. . . Wheareas by the 12 act of assembly held at James City the 3d day of October, Anno Domini 1670, entitled an act declaring who shall be slaves, it is enacted that all servants not being Christians, being imported into this country by shipping shall be slaves, but what shall come by land shall serve if boys and girls until thirty years of age, if men or women, twelve years and no longer; and for as much as many negroes, moors, mullatos, and others borne of and in heathenish, idolatrous, pagan and Mahometan parentage and country have heretofore, and hereafter may be purchased, procured, or otherwise obtained as slaves of, from or out of such their heathenish country by some well-disposed Christian, who after such their obtaining and purchasing such negro, moor, or mulatto as their slave out of a pious zeal, have wrought the conversion of such slave to the Christian faith, which by the laws of this country doth not manumit them or make them free, and afterwards, such their conversion, it hath and may often happen that such master or owner of such slave being by some reason enforced to bring or send such slave into this country to sell or dispose of for his necessity or advantage, he the said master or owner of such servant which notwithstanding his conversion is really his slave, or his factor or agent must be constrained either to carry back or export again the said slave to some other place where they may sell him for a slave, or else depart from their just right and title to such slave and sell him here for no longer time than the English or other Christians are to serve, to the great loss and damage of such master or owner, and to the great discouragement of bringing in such slaves for the future, and to no advantage at all to the planter or buyer; and whereas also those Indians that are taken in war or otherwise by our neighboring Indians, confederates or tributaries to his majesty, and this his plantation of Virginia are slaves to the said neighboring Indians that so take them, and by them are likewise sold to his majesties subjects here as slaves, be it therefore enacted by the governor council and burgesses of this general assembly, and it is enacted by the authority aforesaid, that all the said recited act of the third of October 1670 be, and is hereby repealed and made utterly void to all intents and purposes whatsoever. And be it further enacted by the authority aforesaid that all servants except Turks and Moors, whilst in amity with his majesty which from and after publication of this act shall be brought or imported into this country, either by sea or land, whether Negroes, Moors, Mullattos or Indians, who and whose parentage and native country are not Christian at the time of their first purchase of such servant by some Christian, although afterwards, and before such their importation and bringing into this country, they shall be converted to the Christian faith; and all Indians which shall hereafter be sold by our neighboring Indians, or any other trafficking with us as for slaves are hereby adjudged, deemed and taken, and shall be adjudged, deemed and taken to be slaves to all intents and purposes, any law, usage or custom to the contrary notwithstanding.

Acknowledgments

First and foremost, the authors thank the students who played this game in all its early versions, but especially the first class to play the original prototype and those who contributed substantially to the development of the role sheets and the game's significant elements. Several Reacting instructors reviewed various game iterations and gave invaluable feedback. We deeply appreciate the Reacting community of scholars and friends. Special thanks for the support of various folks at George Fox University: the library staff, including Laurie Lieggi, and the history department administrative assistant, Phyllis Hartle, and her crew of faithful student workers. We are particularly grateful to James Rice, author of *Tales from a Revolution: Bacon's Rebellion and the Transformation of Early America*, who provided constructive criticism that helped us develop the depth and nuance of the game; he has also been an enthusiastic supporter of this project. We are also grateful that the Reacting Consortium featured our game at the annual institute, not just once, but twice, the first time while still a rough prototype. Since that first offering, Nick Proctor and Kelly McFall, successive chairs of the Reacting Editorial Board, have given expert advice on game mechanics and guided *Bacon's Rebellion* from prototype to final product. Without these folks, this Reacting game would never have made it into your hands in published form. Thank you all!

Appendix
March Assembly Proposals

The following is a summary of Berkeley's Proposal/Plan to be voted as law in the March meeting of the Virginia Grand Assembly.

Act I
An Act for the safeguard and defense of the country against Indians.

Whereas this grand assembly hath taken into sad and serious consideration the sundry murders, rapes, and many depredations lately committed and done by Indians on the inhabitants of this country, and the great danger the frontier counties are exposed to by the frequent incursions of Indians, for prevention whereof, and discovering the murders, their aiders and abiders for a full and effectual satisfaction to be taken for them and the future security of the country, Be it enacted and ordained by the Governor, Council, and Burgess of this grand assembly and the authority thereof, that:

- War be declared against Indians who are notoriously known or discovered to have committed the murders, rapings and depredations. And against all other suspect Indians who shall refuse to deliver us such sufficient hostages.
- Charge of war to be borne by the whole country.
- Commission a standing army of 500 men (1/4 horsemen) to be placed at heads of rivers and garrisons at forts.
- Towns must send arms and provisions for four months.
- Each fort captain has the power of impressment for the necessity of the fort.
- Men of military rank in the Assembly also have power to impress.
- Only defense. No offensive attack of Indians shall be made without orders from the Governor.
- Arms can be carried to church and courts in times of danger.
- The Governor has the power to disband the army by timely victory over the enemy.

Act II
An Act prohibiting trade with Indians.

Whereas the country by sad experience have found that the traders with Indians by their avarice have so armed the Indians with powder, shot and guns, that they been thereby emboldened, not only to fall upon the frontier plantations murdered many of our people and alarmed the whole country, but to throw us into chargeable and most dangerous war, and though good laws have been made for prohibiting the trade with Indians for arms and ammunition, yet great quantities have been yearly vended amongst them, for prevention where of for the future. . . .

Be it enacted and ordained by the Governor, Council, and Burgess of this grand assembly and the authority thereof, that:

- If any person or persons whatsoever with this colony from and after 10 days after this present session of assembly shall presume to trade, truck, barter, sell or utter, directly or indirectly, to or with any Indian any powder, shot or arms, except only such as in, and by one proviso hereafter in this act to be appointed and be thereof lawfully convicted shall suffer death without benefit of clergy, and shall forfeit his or their whole estates.
- Felony to be found with them in any Indian town with arms.
- But sober representatives nominated and authorized by courts can trade other goods with neighboring Indians. It is permitted that five persons

from each county chosen by the proper authority to trade with the Indians, except arms.
- Penalty on others not authorized by the assembly—1000 lbs of tobacco, suffered one month imprisoned.

Act III

An act prohibiting the exporting of Corn.

Whereas the country's preparation for war in likelihood may cause a more than ordinary experience of provision, it is there thought fit, it be enacted, and it is by the Governor, Council, and Burgesses of this grand assembly and the authority thereof, enacted and ordained, that no corn or provisions from and after the 5th day of April next, shall be exported out of this colony under the penalty of two hundred pounds of tobacco for every barrel of corn and double the price of any other provision to be paid by the party exporting it.

Notes

CHAPTER 2

1. William S. Powell, "Aftermath of the Massacre: The First Indian War, 1622–1632," *Virginia Magazine of History and Biography* 66, no. 1 (January 1958): 47.

2. Eric Foner, *Give Me Liberty!: An American History* (New York: W. W. Norton, 2014), 1:43.

3. Foner, *Give Me Liberty!*, 52.

4. Ira Berlin, *Many Thousands Gone: The First Two Centuries of Slavery in North America* (Cambridge, MA: Harvard University Press, 1998), 10.

5. Susan Myra Kingsbury, ed., *The Records of the Virginia Company of London* (Washington, DC: United States Government Printing Office, 1933), 3:243.

6. Quoted in Kathleen M. Brown, *Good Wives, Nasty Wenches, and Anxious Patriarchs: Gender, Race, and Power in Colonial Virginia* (Chapel Hill: University of North Carolina Press, 1996), 135–36.

7. Quoted in Edmund S. Morgan, *American Slavery, American Freedom: The Ordeal of Colonial Virginia* (New York: W. W. Norton, 1975), 201.

8. Charles M. Andrews, ed., *Narratives of the Insurrections, 1675–1690* (New York: Charles Scribner's Sons, 1915), 17.

9. Andrews, *Narratives*, 17.

10. William Hand Browne, ed., *Archives of Maryland*, vol. 2, *Proceedings and Acts of the General Assembly of Maryland, April 1666–June 1676* (Baltimore: Maryland Historical Society, 1884), 483.

CHAPTER 5

1. In his correspondence with Sir Edwin Sandys, Rolfe gave a longer version of this arrival: "He [Dutch Captain Jope] brought not any thing but 20. and odd Negroes, which the Governor and Cape Marchant bought for victuals (whereof he was in greate need as he pretended) at the best and easyest rate they could." See Susan Myra Kingsbury, ed., *The Records of the Virginia Company of London* (Washington, DC: United States Government Printing Office, 1933), 3:243.

2. A nearly identical law was passed during Bacon's Assembly, June 1676. Thus, Bacon's loss nonetheless resulted in policy and legal shifts reflecting the values of him and his followers.

Selected Bibliography

"Bacon's Rebellion." *William and Mary Quarterly* 9, no. 1 (July 1900): 1-10.

Berlin, Ira. *Many Thousands Gone: The First Two Centuries of Slavery in North America.* Cambridge, MA: Harvard University Press, 1998.

Berry, John, and Francis Moryson. "Narrative of Bacon's Rebellion." *Virginia Magazine of History and Biography* 4, no. 2 (October 1896): 117-54.

Boles, John B. *Black Southerners, 1619-1869.* Lexington: University Press of Kentucky, 1984.

Breen, T. H., and Stephen Innes. *"Myne Owne Ground": Race and Freedom on Virginia's Eastern Shore, 1640-76.* New York: Oxford University Press, 1980.

Brown, Kathleen M. *Good Wives, Nasty Wenches, and Anxious Patriarchs: Gender, Race, and Power in Colonial Virginia.* Chapel Hill: University of North Carolina Press, 1996.

Carson, Jane. *Bacon's Rebellion, 1676-1976.* Jamestown, VA: Jamestown Foundation, 1976.

Davis, David Brion. *The Problem of Slavery in Western Culture.* Ithaca, NY: Cornell University Press, 1966.

Foner, Eric. *Give Me Liberty!: An American History.* Vol. 1. New York: W. W. Norton, 2014.

Force, Peter, ed. *A List of Those That Have Been Executed for the Late Rebellion, by Sir William Berkeley.* Washington, DC, 1835.

Galenson, David W. *White Servitude in Colonial America: An Economic Analysis.* Cambridge: Cambridge University Press, 1981.

Jordan, Winthrop D. *The White Man's Burden: Historical Origins of Racism in the United States.* Oxford: Oxford University Press, 1974.

Kingsbury, Susan Myra, ed. *The Records of the Virginia Company of London.* Vol. 3. Washington, DC: United States Government Printing Office, 1933.

Morgan, Edmund S. *American Slavery, American Freedom: The Ordeal of Colonial Virginia.* New York: W. W. Norton, 1975.

Parent, Anthony S., Jr. *Foul Means: The Formation of Slave Society in Virginia, 1660-1740.* Chapel Hill: University of North Carolina Press, 2003.

Powell, William S. "Aftermath of the Massacre: The First Indian War, 1622-1632." *Virginia Magazine of History and Biography* 66, no. 1 (January 1958): 44-75.

Rice, James D. "Bacon's Rebellion in Indian Country." *Journal of American History* 101, no. 3 (December 2014): 726-50.

———. *Tales from a Revolution: Bacon's Rebellion and the Transformation of Early America.* New York: Oxford University Press, 2012.

Stanard, Mary Newton. *The Story of Bacon's Rebellion.* Washington, DC: Neale Publishing, 1907.

Tarter, B. "Bacon's Rebellion, the Grievances of the People, and the Political Culture of Seventeenth-Century Virginia." *Virginia Magazine of History and Biography* 119, no. 1 (2011): 1-41.

Washburn, Wilcomb E. *The Governor and the Rebel: A History of Bacon's Rebellion in Virginia.* Chapel Hill: University of North Carolina Press, 1957.

Webb, Stephen Saunders. *1676: The End of American Independence.* Syracuse, NY: Syracuse University Press, 1995.

Wertenbaker, Thomas Jefferson. *Bacon's Rebellion, 1676.* Williamsburg, VA: Virginia 350th Anniversary Celebration, 1957.

Printed in the USA
CPSIA information can be obtained
at www.ICGtesting.com
CBHW081142251024
16405CB00010B/664